英语专业博雅教育课程系列教材

TED
演讲视听说

李丹玲 主编

2

清华大学出版社
北京

内 容 简 介

本教材以TED演讲为素材，精选了14个具有一定代表性的TED演讲，既涉及大学生的学习、生活与成长，也涉及社会热点、历史问题以及值得探讨、辩论的社会现象。每个演讲构成一个单元，每个单元围绕单元演讲主题设计了多种练习题型，以培养提升学生的听说能力。除语言技能外，本教材也注重培养学生用英语进行思考和表达的能力及思辨能力。本教材配有练习参考答案，读者可登录www.tsinghuaelt.com下载使用。

版权所有，侵权必究。举报：010-62782989，beiqinquan@tup.tsinghua.edu.cn。

图书在版编目（CIP）数据

TED演讲视听说. 2 / 李丹玲主编. -- 北京：清华大学出版社, 2025. 2.
(英语专业博雅教育课程系列教材). -- ISBN 978-7-302-68229-5

Ⅰ. H319.9

中国国家版本馆CIP数据核字第2025NQ5483号

责任编辑：刘　艳
封面设计：平　原
责任校对：王荣静
责任印制：刘海龙

出版发行：清华大学出版社
网　　址：https://www.tup.com.cn，https://www.wqxuetang.com
地　　址：北京清华大学学研大厦A座　　邮　　编：100084
社 总 机：010-83470000　　邮　　购：010-62786544
投稿与读者服务：010-62776969，c-service@tup.tsinghua.edu.cn
质量反馈：010-62772015，zhiliang@tup.tsinghua.edu.cn

印 装 者：北京鑫海金澳胶印有限公司
经　　销：全国新华书店
开　　本：185mm×260mm　　印　张：8　　字　数：121千字
版　　次：2025年3月第1版　　　　印　次：2025年3月第1次印刷
定　　价：39.90元

产品编号：100898-01

前　　言

2017年6月，我有幸在清华大学出版社出版了英文教材《TED演讲视听说1》。自出版以来，我陆续收到出版社及读者的来信反馈，给予这本教材良好评价。我没有想到，刚刚站上讲台，将自己的教学素材加以归纳、总结后出版的这本小众教材能够获得国内同行及英语学习者的广泛关注与认可，这对于我来说是莫大的鼓舞。我同时深感惶恐不安：由于教学经验不足、时间短暂及个人能力有限，这部教材还存在改进与提升的空间。

与此同时，社会以及我们的生活每天都在发生改变，除了《TED演讲视听说1》中的热门话题，生活中又涌现了一些值得深入思考与探索的新话题。我需要持续更新教学素材，改进教学方法，才能不断激发学生的求知欲，带给他们新的思考与挑战。

呈现在读者面前的这本《TED演讲视听说2》就是我对以上问题的回应，或者说我的一点小收获。七八年的时光既短暂又漫长，我终于对那些曾经鼓励、温暖我的读者有所回馈，也对自己有所交代。

鉴于很多读者不一定了解TED演讲及我的第一本教材，我有必要对TED演讲及本教材作一点说明。TED的名称来自technology、entertainment和design的首字母，它是美国的一家私有非营利机构，成立于1984年，宗旨是"用思想的力量来改变世界"，以每年3月举行的TED大会而著名。它每年邀请教育、科学、艺术、商业、政治等领域的杰出人物发表演讲，分享他们在各自领域的思考、探索与成就。TED演讲不仅话题丰富，而且观点新颖、深刻、富有启发性，至今已被世界各地的无数观众观看、下载，产生了深远的社会影响，是极为难得的英文学习素材，尤其是英文听说素材。

与《TED 演讲视听说 1》相比，《TED 演讲视听说 2》既有继承，又有改进与提升。本教材在选材思路上一以贯之：选取那些引领时代思潮，关注社会发展，能够带给学生知识、趣味、思考与探索的演讲。这些演讲具有一定的代表性，既涉及大学生的学习、生活与成长，也涉及社会热点、历史问题和值得探讨的社会现象。在单元章节结构方面，本教材有所调整，增加了判断正误和听写填空，删除了写作题，更加注重学生听说能力的提升，也更符合学生由表及里、逐层深入的学习过程。

本教材精选了 14 个 TED 演讲，每个演讲构成一单元，每单元由八部分组成。Part One 为演讲中所涉及的重要词汇。Part Two 为背景知识，包括对演讲人及演讲中涉及的名人、术语的简介。Part Three 为预热问题，与单元演讲主题相关，目的在于启发学生对某一问题进行思考，帮助学生进入积极思维的状态。Part Four 为判断正误，学生在观看第一遍演讲时完成此题，目的在于提升学生从听力材料中获取重要观点、细节的能力。Part Five 为问答题，有些问题源于演讲，有些问题涉及与演讲主旨相关的引申问题。学生在观看第二遍演讲时，应该有意识地关注问题的答案，对于某些重要问题，教师可以组织全班讨论，鼓励学生畅所欲言，提升他们的独立思考及辩证思维能力。Part Six 为听写填空，涉及演讲中的重点、难点、关键词汇。Part Seven 为句子学习，一般为演讲中的重难点句子，学生应该借助上下文语境学习句子中的重点词汇、短语的意义和用法，理解句意，加深对演讲内容的理解。Part Eight 为格言警句，与单元演讲主旨相关。通过阅读这些格言警句，学生不仅能够学到优美、地道的英文，而且能够了解针对同一问题的多种观点，从而活跃思维，开阔视野。

本教材主要供听说课使用，以培养学生的听说能力为主，辅之以其他语言能力的培养。为了给学生提供尽可能多的听说机会，本教材针对每个 TED 演讲设计了多种练习题型。除语言技能外，本教材更强调学生用英语进行思考、表达及思辨的能力。希望 TED 演讲者对于某一话题的独到观点和深刻见解能够带给学生新的知识并提高他们学习的趣味性，引导他们关注社会，唤醒自己内心深处的伟大力量，并且去行动，去改变。

前言

　　本教材每单元至少需要两课时。由于学生的英文水平参差不齐，教师可以针对学生的实际情况，适当安排课时，将课内与课外学习相结合。本教材既适用于高等学校英语专业本科生、英文水平较高的非英语专业本科生和研究生，也可以用于普通英文爱好者系统学习英文。

　　在使用 TED 演讲进行课堂教学时，我常常需要根据学生的具体情况灵活调整，以优化教学效果。在前几年的教学中，我在学生观看完第一遍演讲后，才与其讨论 Part Four 的判断正误题。近两年来，由于短视频的流行，我不得不面对学生注意力下降的问题，在不降低内容质量的基础上，尽量选取时长稍短的演讲。学生观看第一遍演讲时，我会中途暂停，要求学生立即对 Part Four 的句子作出正误判断。学生观看第二遍演讲时，我也会多次暂停，让学生重复观看某些演讲片段，并且立即回答 Part Five 的相关问题。中途暂停和及时、明确的学习任务拉回了学生的注意力，提升了他们的学习效果。对于 Part Eight 的格言警句，我会让学生大声朗读，理解意义，挑选最喜欢的一句，并且与同伴分享原因。学生对于此任务乐此不疲，我总能从他们的发言分享中获得新信息、新观点，还有惊喜与满足。

　　本教材的编写得到了中央财经大学外国语学院及清华大学出版社的大力支持，我对此表示衷心感谢。我还要感谢我的学生。我在本科生的英语听力课及研究生公共英语课程中均用到 TED 演讲，学生不仅对 TED 演讲报以极大的热忱，而且喜欢就演讲中涉及的各种话题展开讨论，发表见解。TED 演讲成为学生独立思考的催化剂，让他们的思想擦出智慧的火花。我喜欢看到学生在获取新知识、新观点时露出的欣喜目光，也喜欢在与学生进行思想交流时获得的小灵感。

　　另外，我将对本教材的音频、视频、参考答案等情况做出说明。本教材无配套的视频，学习者可以登录 TED 官网，通过键入演讲者姓名或者演讲标题搜索到这些演讲。学习者可以在线观看演讲，根据自身需要调整演讲字幕的语种，下载视频、音频，阅读演讲稿。为了提高听力效果，建议学习者在初学过程中关闭字幕。感兴趣的学习者也可以对英文演讲稿进行深入学习。为了弥补《TED 演讲视听说 1》的缺憾，本教材提供 Part Three 至 Part Seven 的参考答案。

最后我想说，社会与时代的发展日新月异，本教材中某些话题热度可能已经有所下降，恳请广大读者谅解。由于时间仓促，能力有限，书中难免有疏漏之处，敬请各位专家、同行批评指正。衷心希望更多人能够从本教材中获益。

李丹玲

2025 年 3 月

CONTENTS

UNIT 1 Time Management **1**

UNIT 2 Social Habits and Networks **9**

UNIT 3 Ghost Stories and Their Grave Truth **17**

UNIT 4 Proactivity and Good Lucks **25**

UNIT 5 The Art of Speaking **33**

UNIT 6 Architecture and Human Relationships **41**

UNIT 7 AIs and Human Fear **49**

UNIT 8 The Epidemic and Its Warning Signals **58**

UNIT 9 Colonialism and Its Aftermaths **67**

UNIT 10 Fat Phobia **76**

UNIT 11 Positivity **85**

UNIT 12 Rejection and Self-Growth **94**

UNIT 13 Big Data and Thick Data **102**

UNIT 14 Human Skin Colors and Revolution **111**

UNIT 1
Time Management

PART ONE
Vocabulary

tardy	(~ in doing sth.) slow to act, move or happen
savor	to enjoy a feeling or an experience thoroughly
shave	to cut a small amount off a price, etc.
errand	a job that you do for sb. and involves going somewhere to take a message, buy sth., deliver goods, etc.
judicious	careful and sensible; showing good judgment
strategy	a plan that is intended to achieve a particular purpose
aftermath	the unpleasant consequence or after-effect of a significant event
triathlon	a sporting event in which people compete in three different sports, usu. swimming, cycling and running
mentor	to advise or train sb., esp. a younger colleague
elastic	able to change or be changed, flexible and adaptable
accommodate	to provide enough space for sb./sth.
priority	sth. that you think is more important than other things and should be dealt with first
equivalent	a person or thing that is equal to or corresponds with another in value, amount, function, meaning, etc.
payroll	a list of a company's employees and the amount of money they are to be paid

intrigued	(~ to do sth.) very interested in sb./sth. and wanting to know more about them
scintillating	very clever, amusing and interesting
doable	able to be done
minimize	to try to make sth. seem less important than it really is
empower	to make (sb.) stronger and more confident, esp. in controlling his/her life and claiming his/her rights
putter	to move or go in a casual, unhurried way
meditate	to think deeply, usu. in silence, esp. for religious reasons or in order to make your mind calm
substitute	(~ for sb./sth.) a person or thing that you use or have instead of the one you normally use or have

PART TWO
Background information

Laura Vanderkam (1978–): She is an American speaker and writer, and has published several books on time management, productivity, work-life balance, and career development. Her articles regularly appear on *The New York Times*, *The Wall Street Journal*, *Fortune* and so on. In her book *I know How She Does It*, she shows how working mothers manage to make balance between careers, family lives and their own passions.

PART THREE
Warm-up questions

Discuss the following questions with your partner and then share your opinions with the whole class.

UNIT 1 Time Management

Do you have problems with managing your time effectively? If so, what are they?

_____

_____

PART FOUR
True or false statements

> Watch the TED talk "How to Gain Control of Your Free Time" by Laura Vanderkam for the first time and decide whether the following statements are true or false.

1. As an expert of time management, Laura is always on time. (   )

2. According to Laura, the idea that we save bits of time here and there, add it up so that we will finally get to everything we want to do is a good method for time management. (   )

3. Time is highly elastic and it will stretch to make room for the activities we choose to put in it. (   )

4. Laura believes that the key to time management is treating our priorities as things we must do. (   )

5. A good way to figure out our priorities is to look backward and make a performance review of the past year. (   )

6. Friday afternoons are the best time to consider putting our priorities into our schedules. (   )

7. People usually work more hours than they claim they do. (   )

PART FIVE
Questions

Watch the TED talk "How to Gain Control of Your Free Time" by Laura Vanderkam for the second time, answer the following questions, and then share your opinions with your partner or the whole class.

1. According to Laura, what are the wrong ideas concerning time held by most people? What are the drawbacks of those ideas?

2. What is the lesson drawn from the busy woman with a broken water heater?

3. For Laura, what is the key to time management? What are the steps of time management?

4. Have you learned any useful lessons from this speech? How will you manage your time effectively in the future?

5. What are your priorities for this semester? Please list your priorities for your study, your relationships, and yourself respectively, and try to break them down into doable steps.

UNIT 1 Time Management

PART SIX
Spot dictation

> Listen to some audio clips and fill in the blanks with the words or phrases you hear.

1. When people find out I write about time management, they _____ two things. One is that I'm always on time, and I'm not. I have four small children, and I would like to blame them for my occasional _____, but sometimes it's just not their fault. I was once late to my own speech on time management. We all had to just take a moment together and _____ that _____.

2. And the idea is that we'll _____ bits of time off everyday activities, add it up, and we'll have time for the good stuff. I question the entire _____ of this piece, but I'm always interested in hearing what they've come up with before they call me. Some of my favorites: doing _____ where you only have to make right-hand turns.

3. I recently did a time diary project looking at 1,001 days in the lives of extremely busy women. They had _____ jobs, sometimes their own businesses, kids to care for, maybe parents to care for, community _____ —busy, busy people.

4. If you've ever had anything like this happen to you, you know it is a hugely damaging, _____, _____ mess. So she's dealing with the immediate _____ that night, next day she's got _____ coming in, day after that, professional cleaning _____ dealing with the _____ carpet. All this is being recorded on her time log. _____ taking seven hours of her week. Seven hours. That's like finding an extra hour in the day.

5. But I'm sure if you had asked her at the start of the week, "Could you find seven hours to train for a _____?" "Could you find seven hours to _____ seven worthy people?"

6. And what this shows us is that time is highly _____. We cannot make more time, but time will stretch to _____ what we choose to put into it. And so the key to time management is treating our _____ as the _____ of that broken water heater.

7. I mean, some people's lives are just harder than others. It is not going to be easy to find time to take that poetry class if you are caring for _____ children on your own. I get that. And I don't want to _____ anyone's struggle. But I do think that the numbers I am about to tell you are _____.

5

PART SEVEN
Sentence study

Read the following sentences and understand their meanings. Pay attention to the bold faced and italic words and phrases.

1. I was once late to my own speech on time management. We all had to just take a moment together and *savor* that *irony*.

2. We'll **shave** bits of time off everyday activities, **add** it **up**, and we'll have time for the good stuff.

3. If you've ever had anything like this happen to you, you know it is a hugely damaging, frightening, *sopping* mess. So she's dealing with the immediate *aftermath* that night.

4. All this is being recorded on her time log. **Winds up** taking seven hours of her week.

5. And what this shows us is that time is highly *elastic*. We cannot make more time, but time will stretch to *accommodate* what we choose to put into it.

6. And so the key to time management is treating our *priorities* as the *equivalent* of that broken water heater.

UNIT 1 — Time Management

7. But the reason she was *unavailable* to speak with me is that she was out for a hike, because it was a beautiful spring morning, and she wanted to go for a hike. So of course this makes me even more *intrigued*.

8. And I don't want to *minimize* anyone's struggle. But I do think that the numbers I am about to tell you are *empowering*.

PART EIGHT
Reading

Read the following quotes and share with others your understanding of them.

1. Don't be fooled by the calendar. There are only as many days in the year as you make use of. One man gets only a week's value out of a year while another man gets a full year's value out of a week. (Charles Richards)

2. It's not enough to be busy, so are the ants. The question is, what are we busy about? (Henry David Thoreau)

3. Lost wealth may be replaced by industry, lost knowledge by study, lost health by temperance or medicine, but lost time is gone forever. (Samuel Smiles)

4. Time is really the only capital that any human being has, and the only thing he can't afford to lose. (Thomas Edison)

5. A wise person does at once, what a fool does at last. Both do the same thing; only at different times. (Baltasar Gracian)

6. One worthwhile task carried to a successful conclusion is worth half-a-hundred half-finished tasks. (Malcolm S. Forbes)

7. Time management is an oxymoron. Time is beyond our control, and the clock keeps sticking regardless of how we lead our lives. Priority management is the answer to maximizing the time we have. (John Maxwell)

8. Give me six hours to chop down a tree and I will spend the first four sharpening the axe. (Abraham Lincoln)

9. The way we spend our time defines who we are. (Jonathan Estrin)

10. Don't spend time beating on a wall, hoping to transform it into a door. (Coco Chanel)

UNIT 2
Social Habits and Networks

PART ONE
Vocabulary

squander	(~ sth. on sb./sth.) to waste money, time, etc. in a stupid or careless way
precipice	a very steep side of a high cliff, mountain or rock
clique	a small group of people who spend their time together and do not allow others to join them
sociologist	a person who studies human societies and the relationships between groups in these societies
redundant	no longer needed or useful
network	a closely connected group of people, companies, etc. that exchange information, etc.; to try to meet and talk to people who may be useful to you in your work
filter	a device through which a substance is passed in order to remove any materials that are not wanted; to pass liquid, light, etc. through a special device, esp. to remove sth. that is not wanted
hub	(~ of sth.) the central and most important part of a particular place or activity
injection	putting a drug or other substance into a person's or an animal's body by using a syringe or similar instrument
constrain	to restrict or limit sb./sth.
harass	to annoy or worry sb. by putting pressure on him/her or saying or doing unpleasant things to him/her

commonality	the state of sharing features or attributes
bully	(~ sb. into sth./into doing sth.) to frighten or hurt a weaker person
ally	a person who helps and supports sb. who is in a difficult situation, esp. a politician
atom	the smallest part of a chemical element that can exist
bond	to establish a relationship or link with sb. based on shared feelings, interests, or experiences

PART TWO
Background information

Tanya Manon: She is Professor of Management and Human Resources at Ohio State University, with a bachelor's degree of sociology from Harvard University and Ph.D. from Stanford Graduate School of Business. She is interested in the mundane feelings and seemingly harmless daily habits that restrict people and cause them to stay in their comfort zone. She also explores the ways that may help people get out of their traps and lead a wider and richer life.

Mark Granovetter (1943–): He is an American sociologist and Professor of Stanford University, famous for the influential article "The Strength of Weak Ties", a widely cited publication in social sciences. He is also associated with the concept of economic sociology "embeddedness", and believes that in market societies, rational economic exchanges are influenced by pre-existing social ties rather than disassociate from them. In 2014, he was selected as the Citation Laureate by Thomson Reuters, a multinational mass media and information company.

PART THREE
Warm-up questions

Discuss the following questions with your partner and then share your opinions with the whole class.

UNIT 2 — Social Habits and Networks

Whom do you usually sit with in class? Do you often sit with the same people or with different people? What are the advantages and disadvantages of this habit of yours?

_____
_____

PART FOUR
True or false statements

Watch the TED talk "The Secret to Great Opportunities? The Person You Haven't Met Yet" by Tanya Manon for the first time, and decide whether the following statements are true or false.

1. Tanya has a superpower of memory, so she sometimes remembers her students' faces, their places in the classroom and the persons whom they sat with even years later. (   )

2. Mark Granovetter found that most people get their jobs through their strong ties—their family or their significant others. (   )

3. To fight our filters means to identify the least interesting people and even the most irritating people and connect with them. (   )

4. In a social hub, we can choose and predict whom we are going to meet, so it requires some planning. (   )

5. By creating a more imprecise social search engine, we can create randomness and luck, which in turn can help broaden our social universe. (   )

6. When threated, low socioeconomic status people would reach out to more people, and think of more people and a broader network. (   )

7. Sentences like "you're a great treasure", "I own you one", and "I'm obliged to you" represent human relations in an economic and transactional way and may make us feel uncomfortable. (   )

PART FIVE
Questions

Watch the TED talk "The Secret to Great Opportunities? The Person You Haven't Met Yet" by Tanya Manon for the second time, answer the following questions, and then share your opinions with your partner or the whole class.

1. According to Tanya's observation, what is her students' habit in class? Why do they do it? What is the danger of it?

2. What is Mark Granovetter's finding concerning "strong ties" and "weak ties"?

3. What are the merits and demerits if we have a predictable network?

4. What are Tanya's strategies for us to break habits that keep us close to home and enlarge our social networks? Can you come up with more ways to broaden your networks?

5. What are the differences of behaviors between low and high socioeconomic status people when they are in a comfortable condition and a threatening one respectively? What do these differences suggest?

6. According to Tanya, what do most of us tend to do when we are at difficult moments and in urgent need of networks? What can we do to counteract such tendency?

UNIT 2 Social Habits and Networks

PART SIX
Spot dictation

Listen to some audio clips and fill in the blanks with the words or phrases you hear.

1. The problem is when we're on a _____, right? When we're in trouble, when we need new ideas, when we need new jobs, when we need new resources—this is when we really pay a price for living in a _____.

2. The first _____ is to use a more _____ social search engine. What I mean by a social search engine is how you are finding and _____ your friends.

3. What I want you to do is find the most _____ person you see as well and connect with them.

4. They're of all different races, all different _____. Maybe people are initially uncomfortable with those roommates, but the amazing thing is, at the end of a year with those students, they're able to overcome that _____ discomfort. They're able to find deep-level _____ with people.

5. And so with these social _____, the _____ is, interestingly enough, to get _____, it requires, actually, some planning.

6. The higher socioeconomic status people thought of more people, they thought of a broader network, they were _____ themselves to _____ back from that _____.

7. We are mentally _____ our networks when we are being _____, when we are being _____, when we are threatened about losing a job, when we feel down and weak.

PART SEVEN
Sentence study

Read the following sentences and understand their meanings. Pay attention to the bold faced and italic words and phrases.

1. They're going to *squander* their chance for an international, diverse network.

2. The problem is when we're on a *precipice*, right? When we're in trouble, when we need new ideas, when we need new jobs, when we need new resources—this is when we really pay a price for living in a *clique*.

3. So if you think about what the problem is with your strong ties, think about your significant other, for example. The network is *redundant*.

4. The other side of it is how we are actually *filtering*. And we do this *automatically*.

5. I force them to work with different people so there are more *accidental bumps* in the network where people get a chance to connect with each other.

6. They're able to find deep-level *commonalities* with people.

7. And so with these social hubs, the *paradox* is, interestingly enough, to get *randomness*, it requires, actually, some planning.

8. And what we found was that our lower socioeconomic status people, when they were comfortable, were actually reaching out to more people. They thought of more people. They were also less *constrained* in how they were *networking*.

UNIT 2 Social Habits and Networks

9. The higher socioeconomic status people thought of more people, they thought of a broader network, they were positioning themselves to **bounce back** from that **setback**.

10. We are mentally **compressing** our networks when we are being **harassed**, when we are being **bullied**, when we are threatened about losing a job, when we feel down and weak. We are **closing** ourselves **off**, isolating ourselves, creating a blind spot where we actually don't see our resources. We don't see our **allies**, we don't see our opportunities.

11. Why not instead think of yourself as an atom, bumping up against other atoms, maybe transferring energy with them, **bonding with** them a little and maybe creating something new on your travels through the social universe?

PART EIGHT
Reading

Read the following quotes and share with others your understanding of them.

1. The currency of real networking is not greed but generosity. (Keith Ferrazzi)

2. Networking is an investment in your business. It takes time and when done correctly can yield great results for years to come. (Diane Helbig)

3. The successful networkers I know, the ones receiving tons of referrals and feeling truly happy about themselves, continually put the other person's needs ahead of their own. (Bob Burg)

4. Your network is your net worth. (Porter Gale)

5. You can have everything in life you want if you will just help enough other people get what they want. (Zig Ziglar)

6. Networking is not about just connecting people. It's about connecting people with people, people with ideas, and people with opportunities. (Michele Jennae)

7. My advice for folks on networking is give, give, give. You will later receive. But you are really planting these seeds. Some of them will die, and they won't become anything. Many of them will take many, many years before they pay off for you if at all. (Sallie Krawcheck)

8. To nurture the sort of relationships that will truly help propel you towards accomplishing great things, you need to forget transactional networking and focus on having in-depth conversations with fewer people about subjects you really care about. (Naveen Jain)

UNIT 3
Ghost Stories and Their Grave Truth

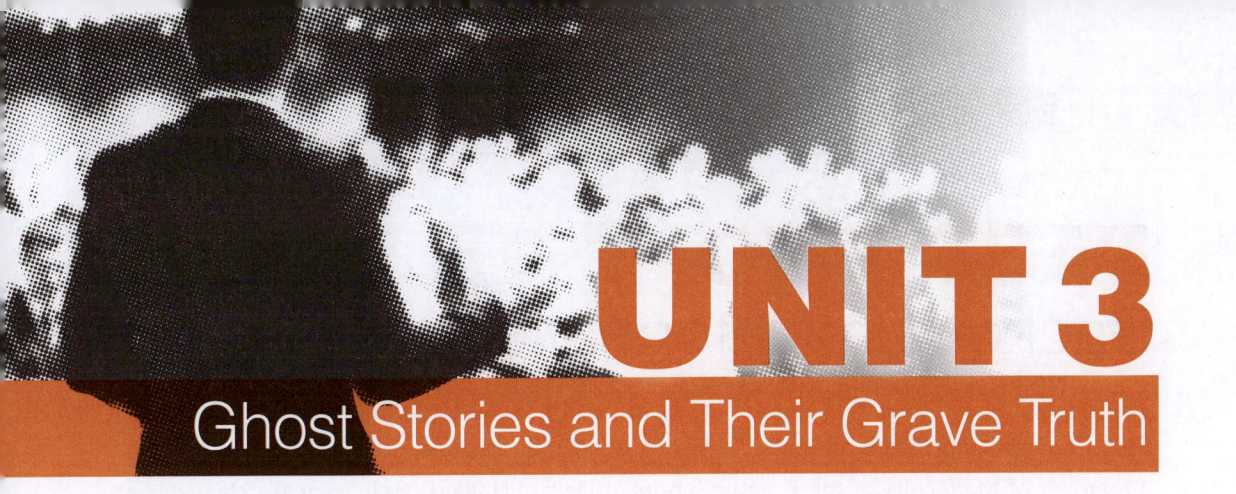

PART ONE
Vocabulary

lynch	(of a group of people) to kill (sb.) for an alleged offence without a legal trial, esp. by hanging
execution	the act of killing sb., esp. as a legal punishment
sanction	to give permission for sth. to take place
lore	the traditional stories and history of a particular culture or field of activity
stance	(~ on sth.) the opinions that sb. has about sth. and expresses publicly
interdisciplinary	involving different areas of knowledge or study
vengeful	showing a desire to punish sb. who has harmed you
ambivalent	(~ about/toward sb./sth.) having or showing both good and bad feelings about sb./sth.
creepy	causing an unpleasant feeling of fear or slight horror
almshouse	a house founded by charity, offering accommodation for poor people
carceral	relating to a prison
appropriate	to take (sth.) for one's own use, typically without the owner's permission
gentrify	to change an area, a person, etc. so that they are suitable for, or can mix with, people of a higher social class than before
prank	a trick that is played on sb. as a joke
mourn	(~ for sb./sth.) to feel and show sadness because sb. has died; to feel sad because sth. no longer exists or is no longer the same

PART TWO
Background information

Coya Paz Brownrigg: She is an American writer, director and scholar. Since 2008, she has been a member of the faculty of the Theater School at DePaul University and teaches classes like directing, history and performance. Currently she also holds the position of Artistic Director of the Free Street Theater in Chicago, believing in the power of theatrical performance for boosting equity among people of difference races. She got her Ph.D. in performance studies at Northwestern University.

Gold Rush California: The Gold Rush in California began from Jan. 24, 1848, when James W. Marshall found gold at Sutter's Mill in Coloma, California. With the discovery of gold, thousands of fortune seekers flooded in California from the U.S. and other countries. The Gold Rush reached its peak in 1852 and by the end of the decade, it was over. It is estimated that over 300,000 people arrived in California, quickening the pace for California to become a state in 1850, and about $2 billion worth of gold was mined.

Chicago Tribune: It is a daily newspaper printed in Chicago, Illinois, a dominant voice of the Midwest and also one of the leading newspapers in the U.S. Founded in 1847 by three Chicagoans, it gained prominence for its coverage of American Civil War and support of Abraham Lincoln under the leadership of Joseph Medill, who was later elected Mayor of Chicago. Over the years, it has won 27 Pulitzer Prizes.

PART THREE
Warm-up questions

> Discuss the following questions with your partner and then share your opinions with the whole class.

Do you have any ghost stories? If so, share your ghost stories with your partner and discuss with them the question: What do you think the ghost(s) want(s)?

UNIT 3 Ghost Stories and Their Grave Truth

PART FOUR
True or false statements

Watch the TED talk "The Haunting Truth of Ghost Stories" by Coya Paz Brownrigg for the first time and decide whether the following statements are true or false.

1. A ghost story about someone being killed and coming back to haunt a town may be one way for the community to pass down its bloody history to future generations. (   )

2. In ghost stories, all ghosts want to be acknowledged. (   )

3. In popular culture, there are both positive and negative portrayals of ghosts. (   )

4. According to *Chicago Tribune,* there are over 380,000 unmarked graves in the back of a Chicago carceral mental hospital. (   )

5. We often find "leave-me-alone" ghost stories in places which are illegally occupied or improperly used. (   )

6. The "are-still-with-us" ghost stories show us how the dead really want to be connected with the living. (   )

7. Coya regards ghost stories as a good conversation starter. (   )

PART FIVE
Questions

Watch the TED talk "The Haunting Truth of Ghost Stories" by Coya Paz Brownrigg for the second time, answer the following questions, and then share your opinions with your partner or the whole class.

1. Why was Coya terrified of ghosts?
   _____
   _____

19

TED 演讲视听说 2

2. What does Coya love about ghost stories?

3. What is the first category of ghost stories? What is the example from Coya to illustrate it?

4. What is your understanding of the category of "leave-me-alone" ghost stories?

5. Who are the ghosts in the "are-still-with-us" category of ghost stories? What does this category reflect about us?

6. What do ghost stories ultimately reveal about us?

7. Which category does your ghost story belong to? What does it reveal about you or people or some communities?

8. Ghost stories are a common phenomenon for people of all nationalities and races, so what are some functions that ghost stories play for us humans?

PART SIX
Spot Dictation

Listen to some audio clips and fill in the blanks with the words or phrases you hear.

UNIT 3 — Ghost Stories and Their Grave Truth

1. I don't know how much you know about _____, but they are, by definition, public _____ that happen off the official record. These deaths aren't technically _____ by the state, and often, towns and communities would deny they even happened.

2. I didn't even want to hear a ghost story because I didn't want to _____ the possibility that a ghost might exist. And why not? In popular culture, ghosts are _____ as mean, _____, destructive forces. They're _____ at worst and _____ at best.

3. I have found that most ghosts fall into one of three categories, and what they all want is pretty much the same—to be _____. The first type of ghost is the kind I started studying. These are the _____ returned.

4. Now, we'd never heard of this mental hospital, and honestly it sounded like any "teenagers breaking into a mental hospital" story you've ever heard—a wheelchair _____ following them, doors _____ shut, _____ laughter.

5. What's interesting to me about this kind of ghost story is that you find it most often in _____ spaces—think _____ neighborhoods or the old "built on a _____ burial ground" trope.

6. So many of us are _____ untimely deaths, and _____ is all around us. Unfortunately, I don't think we're always very good at _____ loss or talking about death, or talking about the way that our history is still living in the present. Ghost stories can be _____, but so is being _____, so is any unknown.

PART SEVEN
Sentence study

Read the following sentences and understand their meanings. Pay attention to the bold faced and italic words and phrases.

1. I don't know how much you know about lynching, but they are, by definition, public **executions** that happen off the official record. These deaths aren't technically *sanctioned* by the state.

2. I didn't even want to hear a ghost story, because I didn't want to **entertain** the possibility that a ghost might exist. And why not? In popular culture, ghosts are portrayed as mean, **vengeful**, destructive forces.

3. Because most people are **ambivalent** about whether or not the ghost actually exists, I ask, "What is it that you want from the ghost?"

4. What's interesting to me about this kind of ghost story is that you find it most often in **appropriated** spaces—think **gentrifying** neighborhoods or the old "built on a sacred burial ground" trope.

5. So maybe there really is a ghost who's trying to push us out, or maybe there's some part of our unconscious that's **grappling with** whether or not we have a right to be here, whether or not we really belong.

6. Maybe they'll tell you a story that **makes the hair** on the back of your neck **stand on end**.

PART EIGHT
Reading

Read the following quotes and share with others your understanding of them.

UNIT 3 — Ghost Stories and Their Grave Truth

1. We tell stories of the dead as a way of making a sense of the living. More than just simple urban legends and campfire tales, ghost stories reveal the contours of our anxieties, the nature of our collective fears and desires, the things we can't talk about in any other way. The past we're most afraid to speak aloud of in the bright light of day is the same past that tends to linger in the ghost stories we whisper in the dark. (Colin Dickey)

2. We fear the dead, when really, we ought to be far more afraid of the living. (A. J. West)

3. Depending on who you ask, sometimes ghost stories are all that is left of history. History is full of ghosts, because it's full of myth. All of it woven together depending on who survived to do the telling. (Roshani Chokshi)

4. We spend a lot of time talking about leaving a legacy in this world, grand or small, financial or repetitional, so that we won't be forgotten. But ghost stories show us a different concern, hidden under our bluster: We hope that the dead won't forget us. We hope that we, the living, will not lose the meanings that seem to evaporate when our loved ones die. (Katherine May)

5. Ghost stories... tell us about things that lie hidden within all of us, and which lurk outside all around us. (Susan Hill)

6. Monsters are real, and ghosts are real too. They live inside us, and sometimes, they win. (Stephen King)

7. A person terrified with the imagination of spectres is more reasonable than one who thinks the appearance of spirits fabulous and groundless. (Joseph Addison)

8. To be haunted is to glimpse a truth that might best be hidden. (James Herbert)

9. Ghosts are never just ghosts; they provide us with an insight into what haunts our culture. (Andrew Smith)

10. Ghosts are a metaphor for memory and remembrance and metaphorically connect our world to the world we cannot know about. (Leslie What)

UNIT 4
Proactivity and Good Lucks

PART ONE
Vocabulary

entrepreneur	a person who makes money by starting or running businesses, esp. when this involves taking financial risks
venture	a business project or activity, esp. one that involves taking risks
gust	a sudden strong increase in the amount and speed of wind that is blowing
binary	based on only two numbers; consisting of two parts
intrigue	to make sb. very interested and want to know more about sth.
loop	a shape produced by a curve that bends round and crosses itself
fellowship	an award of money to a graduate student to allow him/her to continue his/her studies or to do research
gracious	(of people or behavior) kind, polite and generous, esp. to sb. of a lower social position
craft	to make sth. using special skills
tactic	(usu. pl.) the particular method you use to achieve sth.
foster	to encourage sth. to develop
gorgeous	very beautiful and attractive
fabulous	extremely good
leftover	food that has not been eaten at the end of a meal
pitfall	a danger or difficulty, esp. one that is hidden or not obvious at first

ingredient   one of the things from which sth. is made, esp. one of the foods that are used together to make a particular dish

circumstance   the condition of a person's life, esp. the money they have

PART TWO
Background information

Tina Seelig (1957–): She is Professor of Practice in the Department of Management Science and Engineering at Stanford University, and Director of Stanford Technology Ventures Program. Interested in creativity, innovation and entrepreneurship, she explores how we can reframe ideas and come up with bold and innovative ones in some of her classes. She has published 17 books and won several important rewards, including Gordon Prize from the National Academy of Engineering and National Olympus Innovation Award. She got her Ph.D. in neuroscience from Stanford School of Medicine.

PART THREE
Warm-up questions

> Discuss the following questions with your partner and then share your opinions with the whole class.

In daily life, we all wish ourselves good luck. But in reality, we are not always so fortunate and frequently we encounter misfortunes. Do you think it is possible for us to increase our good luck? If so, what can we do to make ourselves luckier?

UNIT 4 Proactivity and Good Lucks

PART FOUR
True or false statements

> Watch the TED talk "The Little Risks You Can Take to Increase Your Luck" by Tina Seelig for the first time and decide whether the following statements are true or false.

1. For Tina, luck is like a lightning strike, isolated and dramatic, rather than the wind, blowing constantly. (   )

2. To increase our luck, we need first to change our relation with ourselves and take some risks. (   )

3. As we grow old, we are more willing to take risks. (   )

4. An emotional risk may mean talking to someone sitting next to us on the train. (   )

5. Tina's book proposal was rejected by a publisher but accepted by his editor and it turned out a best-selling book. (   )

6. To change our relationship with others means helping others. (   )

7. Ideas are either good or bad, and it depends on our judgments. (   )

8. Tina believes that luck is always there and we can do things to catch luck. (   )

PART FIVE
Questions

> Watch the TED talk "The Little Risks You Can Take to Increase Your Luck" by Tina Seelig for the second time, answer the following questions, and then share your opinions with your partner or the whole class.

27

TED演讲视听说 2

1. What is the common sense definition of luck? What is Tina's understanding of luck?
   _____
   _____

2. According to Tina, what is the first thing we need to do to catch good luck?
   _____
   _____

3. Can you figure out some ways to help you get out of your comfort zone?
   _____
   _____

4. What is the second tip from Tina about capturing luck? What is the example from her to illustrate this point?
   _____
   _____

5. What does Tina mean when she says "You want to change your relationship with ideas"? Can you cite specific examples to illustrate the idea?
   _____
   _____

6. What are the terrible experiences you've encountered? Can you transform them into something useful?
   _____
   _____

PART SIX
Spot dictation

> Listen to some audio clips and fill in the blanks with the words or phrases you hear.

1. You see, I teach _____, and we all know that most new _____ fail, and _____ and _____ need all the luck they can get.

28

UNIT 4 Proactivity and Good Lucks

2. But I've realized, by watching so long, that luck is _____ a lightning strike, isolated and dramatic. It's much more like the wind, blowing _____. Sometimes it's calm, and sometimes it blows in _____, and sometimes it comes from directions that you didn't even imagine.

3. I was so taken by the _____ of his message that I invited him to come and meet me. And we spent some time chatting and _____ an idea for an independent study project together.

4. We got to know each other _____ well through that quarter, and he took the project that he started working on in the independent study and turned it, _____, into a company called Play for Tomorrow, where he teaches kids from _____ backgrounds how to, essentially, _____ the lives they dream to live.

5. Over the course of the last couple of years, I've come up with some _____ for my own life to help me really _____ appreciation.

6. So the best ideas are things like a restaurant on a mountaintop with a beautiful sunset, or a restaurant on a boat with a _____ view. And the terrible ideas are things like a restaurant in a _____, or a restaurant with terrible service that's really dirty, or a restaurant that serves cockroach _____.

7. Here's what happens. Within about 10 seconds, someone says, "This is a _____ idea." And they have about three minutes before they _____ the idea to the class.

8. Or the restaurant that's dirty with terrible service? Well, that turns into a restaurant that's a training ground for future _____ to figure out how to avoid all the _____. And the restaurant with cockroach sushi? It turns into a sushi bar with all sorts of really interesting and _____.

PART SEVEN
Sentence study

Read the following sentences and understand their meanings. Pay attention to the bold faced and italic words and phrases.

TED演讲视听说 2

1. I teach entrepreneurship, and we all know that most new *ventures* fail, and innovators and *entrepreneurs* need all the luck they can get.

2. And it becomes clear very quickly to them that risk-taking is not *binary*.

3. He was so *intrigued* by one of the projects the students had done, he thought there might be a book in it, and he wanted to meet those students.

4. And we spent some time chatting and *cooked up* an idea for an independent study project together.

5. He teaches kids from *disadvantaged* backgrounds how to, essentially, *craft* the lives they dream to live.

6. Over the course of the last couple of years, I've come up with some *tactics* for my own life to help me really *foster* appreciation.

7. Or the restaurant that's dirty with terrible service? Well, that turns into a restaurant that's a training ground for future restauranteurs to figure out how to avoid all the *pitfalls*.

UNIT 4　Proactivity and Good Lucks

PART EIGHT
Reading

> Read the following quotes and share with others your understanding of them.

1. Good luck is when opportunity meets preparation, while bad luck is when lack of preparation meets reality. (Eliyahu Goldratt)

2. Diligence is the mother of good luck. (Benjamin Franklin)

3. The golden opportunity you are seeking is in yourself. It is not in your environment; it is not in luck or chance, or the help of others; it is in yourself alone. (Orison Swett Marden)

4. I've found that luck is quite predictable. If you want more luck, take more chances. Be more active. Show up more often. (Brian Tracy)

5. You never know what worse luck your bad luck has saved you from. (Cormac McCarthy)

6. Remember that sometimes not getting what you want is a wonderful stroke of luck. (Dalai Lama XIV)

7. Luck? I don't know anything about luck. I've never banked on it and I'm afraid of people who do. Luck to me is something else: Hard work—and realizing what is opportunity and what isn't. (Lucille Ball)

TED演讲视听说 2

8. The universe works in crazy ways. Your good luck will come in waves, and so does your bad, so you have to take the good with the bad and press forward. (Nick Cummins)

9. The winds and waves are always on the side of the ablest navigators. (Edward Gibbon)

10. Shallow men believe in luck or in circumstance. Strong men believe in cause and effect. (Ralph Waldo Emerson)

UNIT 5
The Art of Speaking

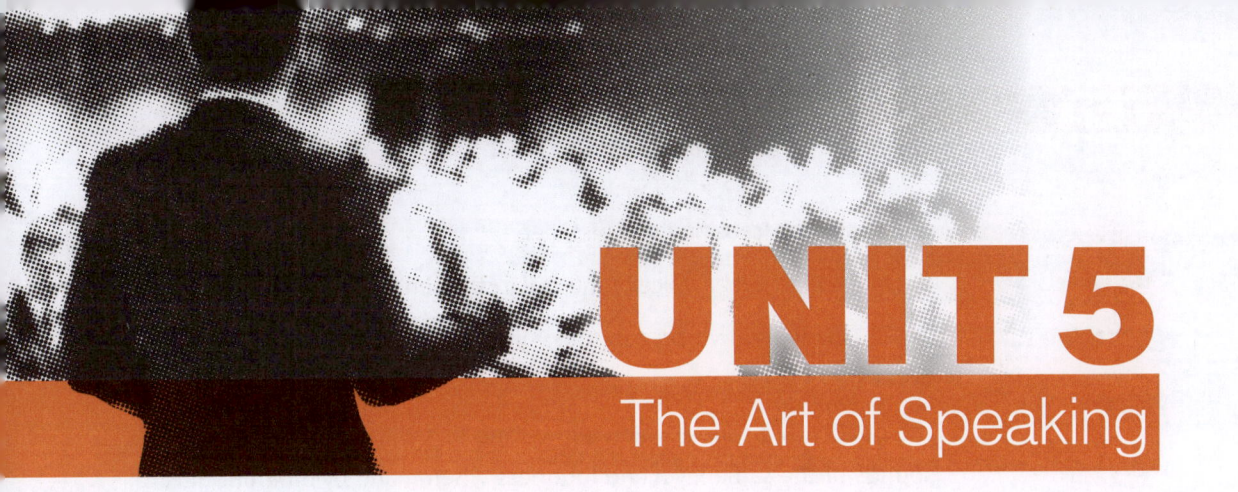

PART ONE
Vocabulary

deadly	likely to cause death
exhaustive	thorough; including all cases or possibilities
dreadful	very bad or unpleasant
viral	like or caused by a virus
penultimate	next/second to the last
embroidery	imaginary details that are added to improve a story
demean	to cause (sb.) to lose his/her sense of personal pride
dogmatism	the quality of holding one's beliefs very strongly and expecting other people to accept them without question
conflate	to bring (parts) together to form a single whole; to combine
bombard	(~ with) to keep attacking heavily (as if) with gunfire
cornerstone	sth. of first importance, on which everything else is based
acclaim	to greet with approval
authenticity	the quality of being true
integrity	strength and firmness of character or principle; honesty; trustworthiness
temper	(~ with) to make less severe by adding sth. else
simultaneous	happening or done at exactly the same time
rummage	an act of turning things over and looking into all the corners while trying

	to find sth. esp. causing great disorder
register	the range of a human voice or musical instrument
falsetto	an unusually high voice, esp. the voice that men use to sing very high notes
timbre	the quality in a sound which allows one to tell the difference between sounds of the same level and loudness when made by different musical instruments or voices
prosody	the rhythmic and intonational aspect of language
singsong	a way of speaking in which a person's voice keeps rising and falling
impart	(~ sth. to sb.) to pass information, knowledge, etc. to other people
monotone	a way of speaking or singing in which the voice neither rises nor falls, but continues on the same note
pitch	the degree of highness or lowness of a musical note or speaking voice
arousal	the act of causing to become active; the state of being active, esp. sexually
acoustics	the qualities of a place, esp. a hall, which influence the way sounds can be heard in it

PART TWO
Background information

Julian Treasure: He is a sound and communication expert, and a speaker of five TED talks about sound and communication with over 100 million times of viewing in total. His talk "How to Speak So That People Want to Listen" is among top ten TED talks of all time. In 2003, he founded The Sound Agency, an audio company to help other companies listen better. He is the author of two books: *How to Be Heard* and *Sound Business* and his mission is to help people and organizations speak powerfully and listen consciously.

Seven Deadly Sins: It is also called the capital vices or cardinal sins. It is the result of classification of sins in Christian tradition, and according to this tradition, the seven sins are pride, greed, wrath, envy, lust, gluttony, and sloth. First compiled by Pope Gregory I around 600 A.D., the seven deadly sins are not clearly listed in *The Holy Bible* but all their concepts can be validated by it.

UNIT 5 The Art of Speaking

PART THREE
Warm-up questions

> Discuss the following questions with your partner and then share your opinions with the whole class.

Do you have experiences that when you speak, people don't listen to you? If so, please discuss with your partner: How can you be a speaker whom people are willing to listen to?

PART FOUR
True or false statements

> Watch the TED talk "How to Speak So That People Want to Listen" by Julian Treasure for the first time and decide whether the following statements are true or false.

1. The human voice is among one of the most powerful sounds in the world. (   )

2. If someone imposes on you a lot of their opinions as if they were facts, such an action is called dogmatism. (   )

3. "Hail" means the stuff that falls from the sky and hits you on the head. (   )

4. According to Julian, most of us speak from our throat. (   )

5. We vote for politicians with higher voices, because we associate higher voices with power and authority. (   )

6. Prosody refers to the way our voices feel, and we prefer voices which are rich, smooth, and warm, like hot chocolate. (   )

7. Silence can be very powerful in talks. (   )

PART FIVE
Questions

> Watch the TED talk "How to Speak So That People Want to Listen" by Julian Treasure for the second time, answer the following questions, and then share your opinions with your partner or the whole class.

1. What are the seven deadly sins of speaking that Julian advises us to avoid? What is your understanding of them?

2. What does "hail" stand for? What are your interpretations of them?

3. Why do we need love to temper our way of speaking?

4. What are the six vocal tools we can use to increase our power of speaking?

5. Can you summarize Julian's suggestions for us to speak powerfully and effectively?

6. Julian says by the end of the talk that "What would the world be like if we were creating sound consciously and consuming sound consciously and designing all our environments consciously for sound?" What does this sentence indicate about the effectiveness of communication among humans?

UNIT 5 The Art of Speaking

PART SIX
Spot dictation

> Listen to some audio clips and fill in the blanks with the words or phrases you hear.

1. I've _____ for your pleasure here seven _____ of speaking. I'm not pretending this is an _____ list, but these seven, I think, are pretty large habits that we can all fall into.

2. _____, the sixth of the seven, _____, exaggeration. It _____ our language, actually, sometimes. For example, if I see something that really is _____, what do I call it?

3. And finally, _____. The _____ of facts with opinions. When those two things get _____, you're listening into the wind. You know, somebody is _____ you with their opinions as if they were true. It's difficult to listen to that.

4. I'd like to suggest that there are four really powerful _____, foundations, that we can stand on if we want our speech to be powerful and to make change in the world. Fortunately, these things spell a word. The word is "_____", and it has a great definition as well.

5. The A is _____, just being yourself. A friend of mine described it as standing in your own truth, which I think is a lovely way to put it. The I is _____, being your word, actually doing what you say, and being somebody people can trust.

6. I love _____. This is the _____, the _____ that we use in order to _____ meaning.

7. People who speak all on one note are really quite hard to listen to if they don't have any _____ at all. That's where the word "_____" comes from, or _____, _____.

37

PART SEVEN
Sentence study

Read the following sentences and understand their meanings. Pay attention to the bold faced and italic words and phrases.

1. I've assembled for your pleasure here seven **deadly** sins of speaking. I'm not pretending this is an **exhaustive** list, but these seven, I think, are pretty large habits that we can all fall into.

2. *Penultimate*, the sixth of the seven, **embroidery**, exaggeration. It **demeans** our language, actually, sometimes.

3. And finally, *dogmatism*. The confusion of facts with opinions. When those two things get *conflated*, you're listening into the *wind*.

4. The I is *integrity*, being your word, actually doing what you say, and being somebody people can trust.

5. *Tempered with* love, of course, honesty is a great thing.

6. I'd like to have a little **rummage** in there with you now and just pull a few tools out that you might like to take away and play with, which will increase the power of your speaking.

7. I love prosody. This is the *singsong,* the metalanguage that we use in order to *impart* meaning.

UNIT 5 — The Art of Speaking

PART EIGHT
Reading

> Read the following quotes and share with others your understanding of them.

1. Think before you speak. Read before you think. (Fran Lebowitz)

2. A good speech should be like a woman's skirt: Long enough to cover the subject and short enough to create interest. (Winston Churchill)

3. The manner of your speaking is full as important as the matter, as more people have ears to be tickled than understandings to judge. (Lord Chesterfield)

4. Nothing in this world is harder than speaking the truth, nothing easier than flattery. (Fyodor Dostoyevsky)

5. Public speaking is the art of diluting a two-minute idea with a two-hour vocabulary. (John F. Kennedy)

6. One must turn the tongue seven times in the mouth before speaking. (Roland Barthes)

7. Only one thing is more frightening than speaking your truth, and that is not speaking. (Naomi Wolf)

8. The most powerful speaking you can do is the speaking that comes from your heart and your love. (Sandra Cisneros)
_____
_____

9. Be still when you have nothing to say; when genuine passion moves you, say what you've got to say, and say it hot. (D. H. Lawrence)
_____
_____

10. Let thy speech be better than silence, or be silent. (Dionysius of Halicarnassus)
_____
_____

UNIT 6
Architecture and Human Relationships

PART ONE
Vocabulary

habitat	the place where a particular type of animal or plant is normally found
sustain	to provide enough of what sb./sth. needs in order to live or exist
precedent	an earlier event or action that is regarded as an example or a guide to be considered in subsequent similar circumstances
egalitarian	based on the belief that all people are equal and deserve equal rights and opportunities
nurture	to care for and encourage the growth or development
horizontal	flat and level; going across and parallel to the ground rather than going up and down
vertical	going straight up or down from a level surface
transition	to undergo or cause to undergo a process or period of changing from one state or condition to another
cohesion	the act or state of keeping together
equity	the quality of being fair and impartial
fortress	a building or place that has been made stronger and protected against attack
perceive	to interpret or regard sb./sth. in a particular way
activate	to make sth. such as a device or chemical process start working
tournament	(in a sport or game) a series of contests between a number of competitors,

	competing for an overall prize
intimidating	frightening in a way that makes a person feel less confident
polarize	to separate or make people separate into two groups with completely opposite opinions
utopian	idealistic, having a strong belief that everything can be perfect, often in a way that does not seem to be realistic or practical

PART TWO
Background information

Jeanne Gang (1964–): She is an American architect, and the founder and leader of Studio Gang, an architecture and urban design practice with offices in Chicago, New York, and San Francisco. She is famous for her design that stresses the relationships among individuals, communities, and the environment. Her approach to design is innovative and inspirational, such as using recyclable materials to conserve resources and increase biodiversity. She earned a bachelor's degree in architecture from University of Illinois at Urbana-Champaign in 1986 and master's degree in architecture from Harvard University in 1993.

PART THREE
Warm-up questions

> Discuss the following questions with your partner and then share your opinions with the whole class.

Do you think buildings and architecture can influence the relationships among people living there? If so, please cite specific examples to illustrate the idea that buildings and architecture either facilitate or prevent human communication.

UNIT 6 Architecture and Human Relationships

PART FOUR
True or false statements

> Watch the TED talk "Buildings That Blend Nature and City" by Jeanne Gang for the first time and decide whether the following statements are true or false.

1. Most people regard architects as relationship builders. (   )

2. Ecologists often think of the interconnection and balance of various species with their environment. (   )

3. In a community meeting house in Mali, the roof makes it possible for people to stand up and take over meetings. (   )

4. In the Arcus Center, there is a kitchen and fireplace, which is a common practice for a building like it. (   )

5. According to Jeanne, tall buildings usually seem isolating and inward, and are not good social connectors. (   )

6. The theoretical basis for "polis station" is that if positive social interactions between the police and the community can be realized, relationships and neighborhood can be reestablished. (   )

7. Jeanne believes that it is possible for public buildings like parks, libraries and schools to become social connectors, but architects need to engage the people using them and reimagine the buildings. (   )

PART FIVE
Questions

> Watch the TED talk "Buildings That Blend Nature and City" by Jeanne Gang for the second time, answer the following questions, and then share your opinions with your partner or the whole class.

TED 演讲视听说 2

1. Why does Jeanne believe that architects are relationship builders?
   _____
   _____

2. What insights can architects get from ecologists?
   _____
   _____

3. How was the Arcus Center designed to break down barriers between social groups and encourage meaningful conversations?
   _____
   _____
   _____

4. How did Jeanne and her team design Aqua to increase social relationships? What are the positive results?
   _____
   _____
   _____

5. How was the police station in North Lawndale in Chicago renovated to rebuild the trust and relationship between the police and citizens?
   _____
   _____
   _____

6. Can we draw any useful lessons from this TED talk about building design?
   _____
   _____

7. Do you think buildings in your university have facilitated relationships among people? If so, in what ways? If not, how should they be improved?
   _____
   _____
   _____

PART SIX
Spot dictation

Listen to some audio clips and fill in the blanks with the words or phrases you hear.

UNIT 6 Architecture and Human Relationships

1. They look at how all the _____ parts of the ecosystem are _____, and it's actually this balance, this web of life, that _____ life.

2. The low roof keeps everybody seated and at equal eye level. It's very _____. I mean, you can't stand up and take over the meeting. You'd actually _____ your head.

3. So we designed a space just like that right in the middle of the Arcus Center, and we _____ it with a fireplace and a kitchen. It's pretty hard to get a kitchen and a fireplace in a building like this with the building _____, but it was so important to the concept, we got it done.

4. The trees _____ carbon when they were growing up, and they gave off _____, and now that carbon is _____ inside the walls and it's not being _____ into the atmosphere. So making the walls is _____ to taking cars right off the road.

5. So I've shown how architecture can connect people on this kind of _____ campus scale. But we wondered if social relationships could be _____—or rather, _____—in tall buildings. Tall buildings don't necessarily lend themselves to being social buildings. They can seem _____ and _____.

6. Engaging the public can be _____, and I've felt that, too. But maybe that's because in architecture school, we don't really learn how to engage the public in the act of design. We're taught to defend our design against _____. But I think that can change, too.

7. So if we can focus the design mind on creating positive, _____ relationships in architecture and through architecture, I believe we can do much more than create individual buildings. We can reduce the stress and the _____ in our urban _____. We can create relationships. We can help _____ this planet we all share.

PART SEVEN
Sentence study

Read the following sentences and understand their meanings. Pay attention to the bold faced and italic words and phrases.

1. They [ecologists] look at how all the diverse parts of the ecosystem are interconnected, and it's actually this balance, this web of life, that *sustains* life.

2. They asked us for a building that could break down traditional *barriers* between different groups and in doing so, create possibilities for meaningful conversations around social justice.

3. There really wasn't a *precedent* for this kind of space, so we looked around the globe and found examples of community meeting houses.

4. The low roof keeps everybody seated and at equal eye level. It's very *egalitarian*.

5. But is it working? Is it creating relationships and *nurturing* them?

6. So I've shown how architecture can connect people on this kind of *horizontal* campus scale. But we wondered if social relationships could be *scaled up*—or rather, upward—in tall buildings.

7. So I've shown how tall buildings can be social connectors, but what about public architecture? How can we create better social *cohesion* in public buildings and civic spaces?

8. So we reached out to community members and police officers in North Lawndale; it's a neighborhood in Chicago where the police station is *perceived* as a scary *fortress* surrounded by a parking lot.

UNIT 6 Architecture and Human Relationships

9. Engaging the public can be *intimidating*, and I've felt that, too.
   _____
   _____

PART EIGHT
Reading

> Read the following quotes and share with others your understanding of them.

1. Architecture arouses sentiments in man. The architect's task, therefore, is to make those sentiments more precise. (Adolf Loos)
   _____
   _____

2. I see my buildings as pieces of cities, and in my designs I try to make them into responsible and contributing citizens. (César Pelli)
   _____
   _____

3. There is a danger when every building has to look spectacular; to look like it is changing the world. I don't care how a building looks if it means something, not to architects, but to the people who use it. (David Chipperfield)
   _____
   _____

4. Architecture should speak of its time and place, but yearn for timelessness. (Frank Gehry)
   _____
   _____

5. The history of architecture is the history of the struggle for light. (Le Corbusier)
   _____
   _____

6. I try to create homes, not houses. (Louis Kahn)

7. The architect must get to know the people who will live in the planned house. From their needs, the rest inevitably follows. (Mies van der Rohe)

8. As an architect you design for the present, with an awareness of the past, for a future which is essentially unknown. (Norman Foster)

9. Here, then, is what I wanted to tell you of my architecture. I created it with courage and idealism, but also with an awareness of the fact that what is important is life, friends, and attempting to make this unjust world a better place in which to live. (Oscar Niemeyer)

10. I don't think that architecture is only about shelter, is only about a very simple enclosure. It should be able to excite you, to calm you, to make you think. (Zaha Hadid)

UNIT 7
AIs and Human Fear

PART ONE
Vocabulary

quintessential	representing the most perfect or typical example of a quality or class
nerd	a foolish or contemptible person who lacks social skills or is boringly studious
sheriff	an elected officer responsible for keeping law and order in a county or town
pastor	a minister in charge of a Christian church or group, esp. in some nonconformist churches
sentient	able to see or feel things through the senses
subjugate	(usu. passive) to defeat sb./sth.; to gain control over sb./sth.
unfounded	not based on reason or fact
humanoid	a machine or creature that looks and behaves like a human
collaborative	involving, or done by, several people or groups of people working together
architect	to design and configure (a program or system)
homicidal	likely to kill another person
emote	to show emotion in a very obvious way
trepidation	great worry or fear about sth. unpleasant that may happen
embody	to express or represent an idea or a quality
discern	to know, recognize or understand sth., esp. sth. that is not obvious

corpus	a collection of written or spoken texts
rogue	(humorous) a person who behaves badly, but in a harmless way
existential	(formal) connected with human existence
insatiable	always wanting more of sth.; not able to be satisfied
dominion	(~ over sb./sth.) authority to rule; control
capricious	showing sudden changes in attitude or behavior
diminish	to become or to make sth. become smaller, weaker, etc.

PART TWO
Background information

Grady Booch (1955–): He is an American scientist and software engineer, and serves as Chief Scientist for Software Engineering at IBM Research. He initiated the term and practice of object-oriented design and is renowned internationally for his contribution to software engineering and architecture. He co-authored the Unified Modeling Language (UML), published six books, and has written numerous articles on software engineering. Recently he is engaged in the development of cognitive systems.

2001: A Space Odyssey: It is a sci-fi movie released on April 3, 1968 in America and directed by Stanley Kubrick. In the movie, the space journey to Jupiter has turned chaotic due to obstruction by HAL, a computer with artificial intelligence. As one of the most influential sci-fi masterpieces, it won several famous awards, including Academy Awards and British Academy Film Awards.

NASA (National Aeronautics and Space Administration): Established in 1958 in response to the former Soviet Union's launch of the first man-made satellite Sputnik in 1957, it is a civilian independent agency of the United States federal government executive branch. Its major responsibilities are to develop and carry out the U.S. space programs, such as aeronautics researches, the launch of satellites, manned and unmanned missions into the space, the training of astronauts, etc. Since its establishment, it has carried out a series of high-profile programs, like Project Mercury, Project Gemini, and Project Apollo.

Alan Turing (1912–1952): He is a British mathematician, logician, cryptanalyst, and computer

UNIT 7 AIs and Human Fear

scientist. From 1931 to 1934, he studied at Cambridge University, and in 1938 he got his Ph.D. from Princeton University. His 1936 seminal paper "On Computable Numbers, with an Application to the Entscheidungs Problem" laid a foundation to the modern computer. During World War II, he took a leading role in decoding wartime ciphers, the German ciphers in particular. In his 1950 paper "Computing Machinery and Intelligence", to create intelligence design standard, he proposed the well-known "Turing Test", which has greatly influenced discussions of and debates over artificial intelligence for the next several decades. He is regarded as the father of computer science and artificial intelligence.

Nick Bostrom (1973–): He is a philosopher and professor at Oxford University, and the director of the Future of Human Institute at Oxford. He has been influential in the concerns and conversations of AIs and in his *The New York Times* bestseller *Superintelligence: Paths, Dangers, Strategies*, he puts forward the ominous idea that "the first ultraintelligent machine is the last invention that man need ever make".

PART THREE
Warm-up questions

> Discuss the following questions with your partner and then share your opinions with the whole class.

AIs have been being developed quickly and used widely. Are you afraid of AIs? Why or why not?

_____
_____

PART FOUR
True or false statements

> Watch the TED Talk "Don't Fear Superintelligent AI" by Grady Booth for the first time and decide whether the following statements are true or false.

1. Grady believes that our fears of AIs are unreasonable and irrational. (   )

2. The Mars is 200 times further away from the Earth than the Moon is, so on average it takes 30 minutes for a signal to travel from the Earth to the Mars. (   )

3. According to Grady, at present it is possible for us to build an AI that has a theory of mind and a moral and ethical foundation. (   )

4. In creating AIs, we can teach them our sense of values and how to distinguish between the good and the evil. (   )

5. In the book *Superintelligence*, the author Dr. Bostrom argues that a system of superintelligence won't be dangerous, nor will it pose a threat to our existence. (   )

6. Grady is confident that an AI controlling every aspect of human life will never happen; for one thing, we can always unplug it. (   )

7. Grady considers it a dangerous distraction that we worry about the rise of superintelligence, for we should at present pay attention to more urgent issues brought by computing. (   )

PART FIVE
Questions

Watch the TED talk "Don't Fear Superintelligent AI" by Grady Booth for the second time, answer the following questions, and then share your opinions with your partner or the whole class.

1. What is HAL?

2. What are the problems for NASA's mission to the Mars? What are the solutions?

UNIT 7 AIs and Human Fear

3. According to Grady, what can scientists do with artificial intelligence? What are they doing now? What must they do?
   _____
   _____

4. Why does Grady not fear AIs?
   _____
   _____

5. What is Dr. Bostrom's idea of superintelligence? What is Grady's response to it?
   _____
   _____

6. After watching this talk, do you feel relieved regarding the potentials of and threats from AIs?
   _____
   _____

PART SIX
Spot dictation

Listen to some audio clips and fill in the blanks with the words or phrases you hear.

1. I grew up in a small town in the dusty plains of north Texas, the son of a _____ who was the son of a _____. Getting into trouble was not an _____. And so I started reading _____ books for fun.

2. Now, HAL was a _____ computer designed to guide the Discovery _____ from the Earth to _____. HAL was also a _____ character, for in the end he chose to value the _____ over human life. Now, HAL was a fictional character, but nonetheless he speaks to our fears, our fears of being _____ by some unfeeling, artificial intelligence who is indifferent to our _____.

3. It became very clear to me that what I needed to _____ was a smart, _____, socially intelligent artificial intelligence. In other words, I needed to build something very much like a HAL but without the _____ tendencies.

4. Now, every new technology brings with it some measure of _____. When we first saw cars, people _____ that we would see the destruction of the family.

5. Indeed, in the book _____ by the philosopher Nick Bostrom, he picks up on this theme and observes that a _____ might not only be dangerous, it could represent an _____ threat to all of humanity. Dr. Bostrom's basic argument is that such systems will eventually have such an _____ thirst for information that they will perhaps learn how to learn and eventually discover that they may have goals that are _____ to human needs.

PART SEVEN
Sentence study

Read the following sentences and understand their meanings. Pay attention to the bold faced and italic words and phrases.

1. When I was a kid, I was the *quintessential nerd*.

2. Now, HAL was a fictional character, but nonetheless he speaks to our fears, our fears of being *subjugated* by some unfeeling, artificial intelligence who is indifferent to our humanity.

3. Another fascinating idea in the mission profile places **humanoid** robots on the surface of the Mars before the humans themselves arrive, first to build facilities and later to serve as *collaborative* members of the science team.

UNIT 7 — AIs and Human Fear

4. What I needed to **architect** was a smart, collaborative, socially intelligent artificial intelligence. In other words, I needed to build something very much like a HAL but without the **homicidal** tendencies.

5. Now, every new technology brings with it some measure of **trepidation**.

6. I do not fear the creation of an AI like this, because it will eventually **embody** some of our values.

7. To teach a system how to play a game like Go, I'd have it play thousands of games of Go, but in the process I also teach it how to **discern** a good game from a bad game.

8. We are not building AIs that control the weather, that direct the tides, that command us **capricious**, chaotic humans.

9. How shall I best organize society when the need for human labor **diminishes**?

PART EIGHT
Reading

Read the following quotes and share with others your understanding of them.

1. The development of full artificial intelligence could spell the end of the human race… It would take off on its own, and re-design itself at an ever increasing rate. Humans, who are limited by slow biological evolution, couldn't compete, and would be superseded. (Stephen Hawking)

2. I visualize a time when we will be to robots what dogs are to humans, and I'm rooting for the machines. (Claude Shannon)

3. The real question is, when will we draft an artificial intelligence bill of rights? What will that consist of? And who will get to decide that? (Gray Scott)

4. Some people call this artificial intelligence, but the reality is this technology will enhance us. So instead of artificial intelligence, I think we'll augment our intelligence. (Ginni Rometty)

5. By far, the greatest danger of artificial intelligence is that people conclude too early that they understand it. (Eliezer Yudkowsky)

6. With artificial intelligence, we are summoning the demon. You know all those stories where there's the guy with the pentagram and the holy water, and he's like, yeah, he's sure he can control the demon? Doesn't work out. (Elon Musk)

7. I believe this artificial intelligence is going to be our partner. If we misuse it, it will be a risk. If we use it right, it can be our partner. (Masayoshi Son)

UNIT 7 AIs and Human Fear

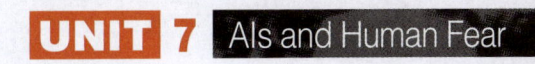

8. Advances in automation, artificial intelligence and robotics, while increasing productivity, will also cause major upheavals to the workforce. (John Hickenlooper)

9. The purest case of an intelligence explosion would be an artificial intelligence rewriting its own source code. The key idea is that if you can improve intelligence even a little, the process accelerates. It's a tipping point. Like trying to balance a pen on one end—as soon as it tilts even a little, it quickly falls the rest of the way. (Eliezer Yudkowsky)

UNIT 8
The Epidemic and Its Warning Signals

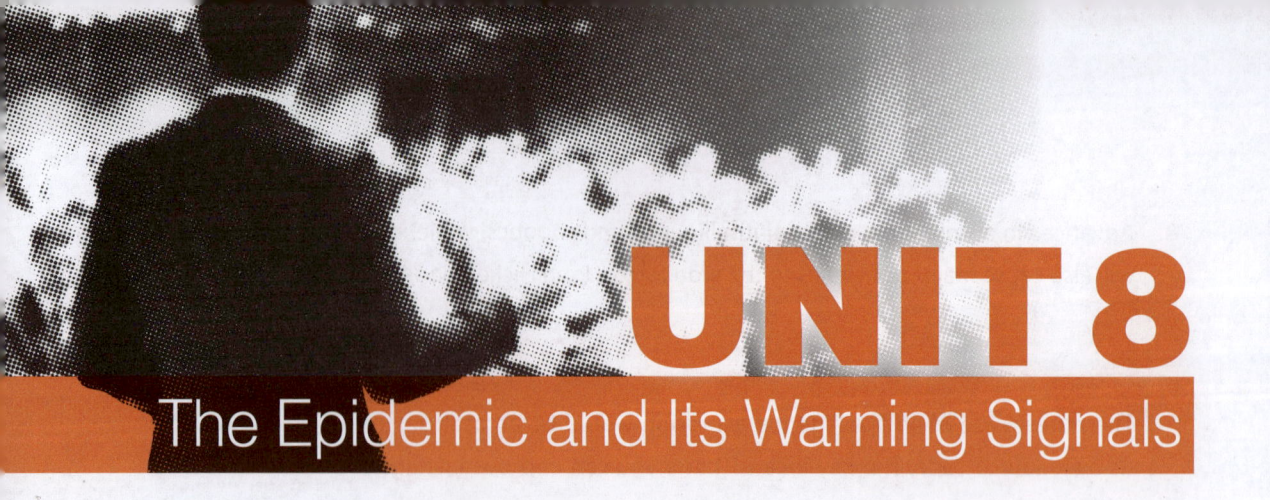

PART ONE
Vocabulary

hunker	to squat or crouch down low
catastrophe	a sudden event that causes many people to suffer
microbe	an extremely small living thing that may cause disease
deterrent	(~ to sb. /sth.) a thing that makes sb. less likely to do sth.
epidemic	a large number of cases of a particular disease happening at the same time in a particular community
eradicate	to destroy or get rid of sth. completely, esp. sth. bad
orchestrate	to plan or coordinate the elements of (a situation) to produce a desired effect
diagnostics	the practice or methods of finding out what is wrong with a person who is sick
plasma	the clear liquid part of blood, in which the blood cells, etc. float
devastating	causing a lot of damage and destruction, disastrous
bedridden	confined to bed by sickness or old age
pathogen	a thing that causes disease
turnaround	a situation in which sth. changes from bad to good
deploy	to move soldiers or weapons into a position where they are ready for military action; to use sth. effectively
logistics	the practical organization that is needed to make a complicated plan

UNIT 8 The Epidemic and Its Warning Signals

	successful when a lot of people and equipment are involved
germ	a very small living thing that can cause infection and disease
simulation	a situation in which a particular set of conditions is created artificially in order to study or experience sth. that could exist in reality
equity	a situation in which everyone is treated equally
hoard	to collect and keep large amounts of food, money, etc., esp. secretly

PART TWO
Background information

Bill Gates (1955–): As an American entrepreneur, inventor and philanthropist, Bill Gates is one of the richest and most influential people in the world. He entered Harvard University in 1973, but dropped out of it in 1975 to build Microsoft—the world largest software company—with his childhood friend Paul Allen. He served as CEO and Chairman of Microsoft until in 2014 when he stepped down, but he remains on the board and works as the technology advisor of it. In 2000 Gates and his then wife Melinda established the Bill & Melinda Gates Foundation, committed to various charitable activities and programs. He has changed the world through his technological innovation, business strategies and philanthropy, and was named by the *Time Magazine* as "one of the 100 people who most influenced the 20th century".

NATO (The North Atlantic Treaty Organization): Founded after World War II in 1949, it is an intergovernmental military organization among European and North American countries. It was originally established as a defense against the threat from the Soviet Union. Currently, there are 30 countries, including the Great Britain, France, Germany, Canada, and the United States. Its missions are to protect the freedom of its member countries, and to stop weapons of mass destruction, cyber-attacks, and terrorism.

Ebola (Ebola Virus Disease): It is a deadly and contagious disease in humans and non-human primates. The viruses that cause Ebola are mainly located in Sub-Saharan Africa. Humans can get Ebola through direct contact with infected animals or humans. It was first identified in 1976, but scientists believe that Ebola virus existed long before its first recorded outbreak. Symptoms of it include fever, aches, pains, weakness, fatigue, bleeding, bruise, red eyes, skin rash, etc.

World Bank (World Bank Group): It is an international organization affiliated with the United Nations (UN). Founded in 1944 at the UN Monetary and Financial Conference and headquartered in Washington D.C., it has 189 member countries, with missions to end extreme poverty and promote shared prosperity among members. It plays an important role in providing finances, policy advice and technical assistance to developing countries.

PART THREE
Warm-up questions

Discuss the following questions with your partner and then share your opinions with the whole class.

1. Do you know any of the deadliest outbreaks of epidemics in human history?

2. Giving the frequent occurrence of epidemics, what can we do to prevent/reduce their outbreaks?

PART FOUR
True or false statements

Watch the TED talk "The Next Outbreak? We're Not Ready" by Bill Gates for the first time and decide whether the following statements are true or false.

1. As a kid, what Bill worried most was a highly infectious virus. (   )

2. A major task of the WHO is to monitor epidemics. (   )

UNIT 8　The Epidemic and Its Warning Signals

3. Bill thinks it lucky that the 2014 Ebola did not spread into many urban areas. (　)

4. In 1918, over 300 million people died from the Spanish Flu. (　)

5. The World Bank estimates that if we have a worldwide flu epidemic, global wealth will go down by over three billion dollars. (　)

6. The last germ game organized in the United States in 2001 went very well. (　)

7. The cost for getting ready for the next epidemic will be very expensive. (　)

8. The positive thing of Ebola is that it serves as an early warning for us to get ready for the next epidemic. (　)

PART FIVE
Questions

> Watch the TED Talk "The Next Outbreak? We're Not Ready" by Bill Gates for the second time, answer the following questions, and then share your opinions with your partner or the whole class.

1. According to Bill, what is the greatest risk we face today? Why does he think so?

2. What were the problems we encountered when we dealt with Ebola in 2015?

3. Why did Ebola not spread to more countries?

4. What are the advantages we have already had when we build a good virus response system?

5. What can we learn from a war when we get prepared for an epidemic?

6. What are the keys to getting ready for the next epidemic?

7. Bill warned us to get ready for the next epidemic as early as in 2015, but from the outbreak of the COVID-19 pandemic, it seems that we have not listened to him. Why do you think this is the case?

8. What are the short-term and long-term effects of the COVID-19 pandemic? And what are the profound lessons it teaches us?

PART SIX
Spot dictation

Listen to some audio clips and fill in the blanks with the words or phrases you hear.

1. Today the greatest risk of global _____ doesn't look like this. Instead, it looks like this... If anything kills over 10 million people in the next few decades, it's most likely to be a highly _____ virus rather than a war. Not _____, but _____. Now, part of the reason for this is that we've invested a huge amount in nuclear _____. But we've actually invested very little in a system to stop an epidemic. We're not ready for the next epidemic.

2. The best lessons, I think, on how to get prepared are again, what we do for war. For soldiers, we have full-time, waiting to go. We have _____ that can _____ to large numbers. NATO has a _____ unit that can _____ very rapidly. NATO does a lot of war games to check, are people well trained? Do they understand about _____ and _____ and the same radio _____? So they are absolutely ready to go. So those are the kinds of things we

UNIT 8 The Epidemic and Its Warning Signals

need to deal with an epidemic.

3. Now I don't have an exact _____ for what this would cost, but I'm quite sure it's very modest compared to the potential harm. The World Bank estimates that if we have a worldwide _____ epidemic, global wealth will go down by over three _____ dollars and we'd have millions and millions of deaths. These investments offer significant benefits beyond just being ready for the epidemic. The primary _____, the R&D, those things would reduce global health _____ and make the world more just as well as more safe.

4. So I think this should absolutely be a _____. There's no need to _____. We don't have to _____ cans of spaghetti or go down into the basement. But we need to get going, because time is not on our side.

PART SEVEN
Sentence study

> Read the following sentences and understand their meanings. Pay attention to the bold faced and italic words and phrases.

1. Today the greatest risk of global **catastrophe** doesn't look like this. Instead, it looks like this. If anything kills over 10 million people in the next few decades, it's most likely to be a highly *infectious* virus rather than a war. Not missiles, but microbes. Now, part of the reason for this is that we've invested a huge amount in nuclear **deterrents**.

2. Now, Médecins Sans Frontières did a great job *orchestrating* volunteers.

3. The failure to prepare could allow the next epidemic to be dramatically more *devastating* than Ebola.

4. Ebola does not spread through the air. And by the time you're **contagious**, most people are so sick that they're **bedridden**.

5. We have **reserves** that can **scale** us **up** to large numbers. NATO has a mobile unit that can **deploy** very rapidly.

6. We need to do **simulations**, germ games, not war games, so that we see where the holes are.

PART EIGHT
Reading

> Read the following quotes and share with others your understanding of them.

1. All countries should immediately now activate their pandemic preparedness plans. Countries should remain on high alert for unusual outbreaks of influenza-like illness and severe pneumonia. (Margaret Chen)

2. You have to find a way to respect these new boundaries (related to coronavirus), but still live the version of life you're used to. That's what life is, regardless of circumstance. (Caroline Wright)

UNIT 8 The Epidemic and Its Warning Signals

3. This virus is creating new ways for everyone to think of how to keep your family and friends safe. We are in uncharted territory and we will all learn together. At one time I did not know how much time our family would have together. So I have gratitude now for every day that we get to be together. (Christin Gigstad)

4. We have a chance to do something extraordinary. As we head out of this pandemic (COVID-19) we can change the world. Create a world of love. A world where we are kind to each other. A world where we are kind no matter what class, race, sexual orientation, what religion or lack of or what job we have. A world we don't judge those at the food bank because that may be us if things were just slightly different. Let love and kindness be our roadmap. (Johnny Corn)

5. This pandemic (COVID-19) is unprecedented for us, but we have experienced other hard things. This time gives us an opportunity to practice resilience and to show our kids what resilience looks like. (Audrey Monke)

6. The pandemic (COVID-19) has been such an awful time for so many people around the world, but it has also been a reminder for us about the things that really matter—the people in our lives and the love we have for them. (Ananya Birla)

7. Pandemic influenza is by nature an international issue; it requires an international solution. (Margaret Chan)

8. The COVID-19 pandemic has demonstrated that infectious diseases know no borders. (Abigail Spanberger)

9. That the AIDS pandemic is threatening sustainable development in Africa only reinforces the reality that health is at the center of sustainable development. (Gro Harlem Brundtland)

10. There's never been a pandemic which hasn't exploited a change in the way we live—politics, social structure, technological change, warfare. It's always something that we humans have done or are doing that's tilled the soil for the pandemic and the solution to it is usually social, behavioural and political. (Norman Swan)

11. Without equity, pandemic battles will fail. Viruses will simply recirculate, and perhaps undergo mutations or changes that render vaccines useless, passing through the unprotected populations of the planet. (Laurie Garrett)

UNIT 9
Colonialism and Its Aftermaths

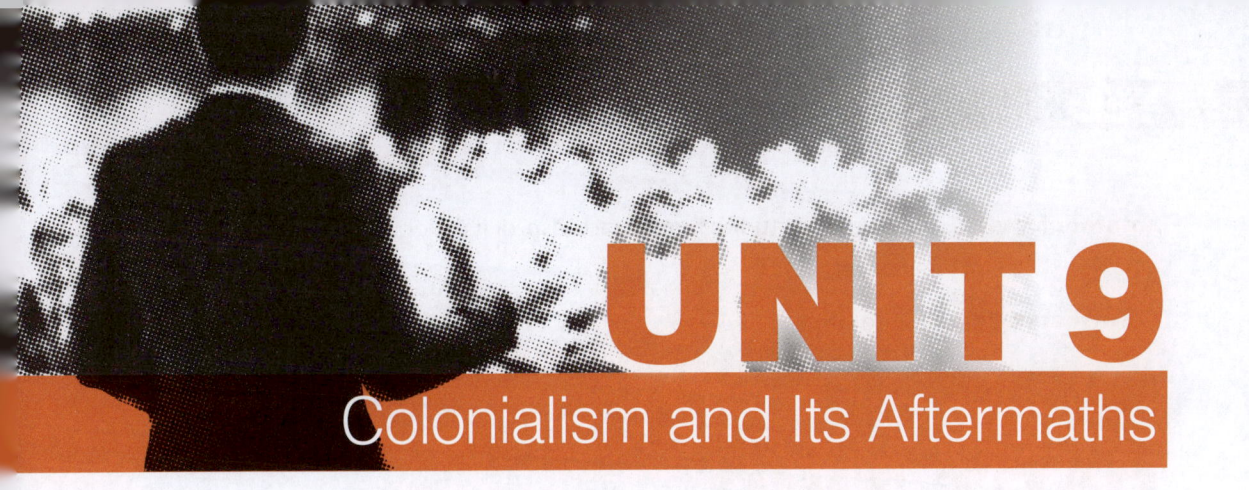

PART ONE
Vocabulary

colonial	relating to or characteristic of a colony or colonies
rose-tinted	rose-colored, of a warm pink color, used in reference to naively optimistic or idealistic viewpoint
benevolent	kind, helpful and generous
murky	dark and gloomy, obscure or morally questionable
cognitive	connected with mental process of understanding
therapy	the treatment of a physical problem or an illness
phobia	a strong unreasonable fear of sth.
misogyny	the hatred of women by men
campaign	(~ against/for sth.) a series of planned activities that are intended to achieve a particular social, commercial or political aim
residual	remaining at the end of a process
trope	a figurative or metaphorical use of a word or expression
interrogate	to ask questions of (sb.) closely, aggressively, or formally
exotic	from or in another country, esp. a tropical one
genesis	the beginning or origin of sth.
contestation	the action or process of disputing or arguing
staid	boring and old-fashioned

anthropologist a person who studies human race, esp. of its origin, development, customs and beliefs

notwithstanding despite sth.

PART TWO
Background information

Farish Ahmad-Noor (1967–): He is a Malaysian political scientist and historian, and currently a senior fellow at the S. Rajaratnam School of International Studies (RSIS) at Nanyang Technological University in Singapore and an affiliated professor at Universitas Muhamadiyah Surakarta (UMS), Indonesia. One of his research areas is the history of Southeast Asia in the 19th century. He is especially interested in the impacts of colonialism on Asia and believes that colonialism is not simply a form of violent conquest, but its influence upon people's mind has been subtle and persisting.

PART THREE
Warm-up questions

Discuss the following questions with your partner and then share your opinions with the whole class.

1. Could you please use your own words to explain the term "colonialism"?
   _____
   _____

2. Do you know the history of colonialism worldwide since the modern times?
   _____
   _____

UNIT 9 Colonialism and Its Aftermaths

3. What are the aftermaths of colonialism?

    _____

    _____

PART FOUR
True or false statements

Watch the TED talk "Why Is Colonialism Still Romanticized?" by Farish Ahmad-Noor for the first time and decide whether the following statements are true or false.

1. Some people in Asia still hold the opinion that colonialism is a good thing. (   )

2. If Farish were living in the 19th century colonial Southeast Asia, he would still be a professor. (   )

3. Historians can get into people's internal mental universe and change their ideas. (   )

4. The fact that some prejudices such as misogyny, racism and various kinds of phobia persist is partly because people rely on a small pool of basic ideas which don't get challenged. (   )

5. Southeast Asians represent their society with some obligatory elements, such as coconut trees, banana trees and orangutan. (   )

6. Traditionally, Southeast Asians regard nature as something to be exploited and defeated. (   )

7. Southeast Asians tend to exoticize themselves till today. (   )

8. Farish believes that historians need to work with people from other fields, such as physics, chemistry, biology and so on. (   )

PART FIVE
Questions

Watch the TED talk "Why Is Colonialism Still Romanticized?" by Farish Ahmad-Noor for the second time, answer the following questions, and then share your opinions with your partner or the whole class.

1. What has been puzzling Farish, a historian, for a long time?

2. Why has Farish been increasingly drawn to psychology and cognitive behavioral therapy over the last few years?

3. How are people from the countryside represented in Southeast Asian sitcoms? What is the origin of such portrayal?

4. Why does Farish believe that he cannot work alone?

5. Why are Southeast Asians still living in the long shadow of the 19th century?

6. Do you think some of our ideas of ourselves are also under the influence of Westerners' stereotypes of us? If so, what are your specific examples? How can we get rid of those stereotypes and not be trapped by them?

UNIT 9 Colonialism and Its Aftermaths

PART SIX
Spot dictation

> Listen to some audio clips and fill in the blanks with the words or phrases you hear.

1. And in particular, I'm interested to understand why some people—not all, by no means—but some people in _____ Asia still hold on to a somewhat _____ view of the colonial past, see it through kind of rose-tinted _____ as perhaps a time that was _____ or nice or pleasant, even though historians know the realities of the violence and the _____ and the darker side of that entire colonial experience.

2. I'm increasingly drawn to things like psychology and _____ behavioral _____; because in these fields, scholars look at the _____ of ideas. Why do some people have certain prejudices? Why are there certain biases, certain _____?

3. We live, unfortunately, sadly, in a world where, still, _____ persists, _____ persists, all kinds of _____.

4. So the way in which we live in our part of the world, postcolonial Southeast Asia, in so many ways, for me, bears _____ traces to ideas, _____, _____, _____ that have a history.

5. I can't work alone anymore, because there's absolutely no point in me doing my _____ work, there's no point in me _____ the roots of these ideas, tracing the _____ of ideas and then putting it in some journal to be read by maybe three other historians.

PART SEVEN
Sentence study

> Read the following sentences and understand their meanings. Pay attention to the bold faced and italic words and phrases.

71

1. But some people in postcolonial Asia still hold on to a somewhat romanticized view of the colonial past, see it through kind of *rose-tinted* lenses as perhaps a time that was *benevolent* or nice or pleasant.

2. There're still some quarters that somehow want to hold on to this idea that that past was not as *murky*, that there was a romanticized side to it.

3. We live, unfortunately, sadly, in a world where, still, *misogyny persists*, racism persists, all kinds of *phobias*.

4. I think it's good that tourists come to Southeast Asia, because it's *part and parcel of* broadening your worldview and meeting cultures, etc.

5. But look at how we represent ourselves through the tourist campaigns, the tourist ads that we produce. There will be the *obligatory* coconut tree, banana tree, orangutan.

6. We've turned Southeast Asian identity into a kind of *cosplay*… And we *parade* this identity, not asking ourselves how and when did this particular image of ourselves emerge.

7. There's no point in me seeking the roots of these ideas, tracing the *genesis* of ideas and then putting it in some journal to be read by maybe three other historians.

8. But for us to adapt to this change, for us to be ready for that change, we need to think out of the box, and we can't fall back, we can't *fall back on* the same set of clichéd, tired, staid old stereotypes.

UNIT 9 Colonialism and Its Aftermaths

9. But rather there are many other histories, many other ideas that were forgotten, *marginalized*, erased along the line.

10. And the person might then come to the conclusion that, well, *notwithstanding* the fact that colonialism is over, we are still in so, so many ways living in the long shadow of the 19th century.

PART EIGHT
Reading

Read the following quotes and share with others your understanding of them.

1. We in the West must bear in mind that the poor countries are poor primarily because we have exploited them through political or economic colonialism. (Martin Luther King, Jr.)

2. But colonialism in its harshest forms is not only the exploitation of new nations by old, of dark skins by light, or the subjugation of the poor by the rich. My nation was once a colony, and we know what colonialism means; the exploitation and subjugation of the weak by the powerful, of the many by the few, of the governed who have given no consent to be governed, whatever their continent, their class, their color. (John F. Kennedy)

3. The native must realize that colonialism never gives anything away for nothing. (Frantz Fanon)

4. Africa is a paradox which illustrates and highlights neo-colonialism. Her earth is rich, yet the products that come from above and below the soil continue to enrich, not Africans predominantly, but groups and individuals who operate to Africa's impoverishment. (Kwame Nkrumah)

5. The essence of neo-colonialism is that the state which is subject to it is, in theory, independent and has all the outward trappings of international sovereignty. In reality its economic system and thus its political policy is directed from outside. (Kwame Nkrumah)

6. The history of colonialism is long and bloody. And it continues today, in the shape of Western arrogance vis-à-vis everyone else. "Us against the rest of the world" is the formula that drives the West. (Abdul Sattar Abu Risha)

7. Colonialism subdues in many dulcet guises. It conquered under the pretext of spreading Christianity, civilization, law and order, to make the world safe for democracy. (F. Sionil Jose)

8. A state in the grip of neo-colonialism is not master of its own destiny. It is this factor which makes neo-colonialism such a serious threat to world peace. (Kwame Nkrumah)

9. Colonialism is the massive fog that has clouded our imaginations regarding who we could be, excised our memories of who we once were, and numbed our understanding of our current existence. (Waziyatawin)

UNIT 9 Colonialism and Its Aftermaths

10. Our colonizers have taught us to believe that our health has improved because of Western medicine, Western foods, and Western technology. In a society that values progress, our colonizers taught us that conditions in the world are perpetually improving, that with each new technological advancement, each new discovery, each new way to utilize resources, each new way to alter the environment, that the world is getting better, that it is advancing. These are all lies. (Waziyatawin)

UNIT 10
Fat Phobia

PART ONE
Vocabulary

relentless	not stopping or getting less strong
chubby	slightly fat in a way that people usually find attractive
cuddly	endearing and pleasant to cuddle, esp. as a result of being soft or plump
voluptuous	(of a woman) attractive in a sexual way with large breasts and hips
curvaceous	(esp. of a woman or a woman's figure) having an attractive curved shape
sugarcoat	to do sth. that makes an unpleasant situation seem less unpleasant
hilarious	extremely funny
diabetes	a disorder of the metabolism causing excessive thirst and the production of large amounts of urine
carb	(short for carbohydrate) a substance such as sugar or starch that consists of carbon, hydrogen and oxygen; (pl.) foods such as bread, potatoes and rice that contain a lot of carbohydrate
renew	to begin sth. again after a pause or an interruption
insidious	spreading gradually or without being noticed, but causing serious harm
patriarchy	a society, system or country that is ruled or controlled by men
ingrained	(of a habit, an attitude, etc.) that has existed for a long time and is therefore difficult to change
disdain	(~ for sb./sth.) the feeling that sb./sth. is not good enough to deserve your respect or attention

UNIT 10 Fat Phobia

subscribe	(~ to) to express or feel agreement with (an idea or proposal)
arbitrary	based on random choice or personal whim, rather than any reason or system
tutu	a ballet dancer's skirt made of many layers of material
deprogram	to release (sb.) from apparent brainwashing, typically that of a religious cult
holistic	considering a whole thing or being to be more than a collection of parts
academic	a person who teaches and/or does research at a university or college
status quo	(Latin) the situation as it is now, or as it was before a recent change
antidote	(~ to sth.) a substance that controls the effects of a poison or disease; anything that takes away the effects of sth. unpleasant
contour	to mould into a specific shape, esp. one designed to fit into sth. else
prohibitive	preventing people from doing sth. by law
en masse	(French) all together, and usu. in large numbers
synchronize	(~ sth. with sth.) to happen at the same time or to move at the same speed as sth.
defiant	openly refusing to obey sb./sth., sometimes in an aggressive way
stamina	the physical or mental strength that enables you to do sth. difficult for long periods of time
rave	(also rave review) an article in a newspaper or magazine that is very enthusiastic about a particular film, book, etc.
detractor	a person who tries to make sb./sth. seem less good or valuable by criticizing it
glorify	(often disapproving) to make sth. seem better or more important than it really is
myriad	an extremely large number of sth.

PART TWO
Background information

Kelli Jean Drinkwater: She is a filmmaker, artist and activist, known for her artistic activities and voice in radical body politics. She uses the body as a site and medium to probe into themes like our relationship with our bodies and society's fear of the fat body and obsession with perfection. Her TED talk "Enough with the Fear of Fat" (2016) was presented at the Sydney Opera House and till now has over 2 million views. She has a B.A. in visual art from University of Newcastle, and has also studied at University of California at Irvine.

Beth Ditto (1981–): She is an American actress and singer-songwriter, and was the lead singer of the band Gossip until its dissolution in 2016. She is an open lesbian, and is famous for challenging the public perceptions of female beauty and sexuality.

PART THREE
Warm-up questions

> Discuss the following questions with your partner and then share your opinions with the whole class.

1. Are you afraid of putting on weight or being fat? Why or why not?

2. Do you think there exist some biases against fat people in our society?

UNIT 10 Fat Phobia

PART FOUR
True or false statements

Watch the TED talk "Enough with the Fear of Fat" by Kelli Jean Drinkwater for the first time and decide whether the following statements are true or false.

1. Some industries are prosperous out of people's fear of being fat. (   )

2. Fat phobia can be directed at individuals and groups, but not ourselves. (   )

3. Fat phobia is a form of systematic oppression, unrelated to capitalism, patriarchy or racism. (   )

4. Kelli has been laughed at, abused, and encouraged by strangers because of her fatness. (   )

5. For Kelli, mental health, self-worth and how people feel in their bodies are as important as numbers on the BMI (Body Mass Index) chart. (   )

6. Kelli believes that fatties reclaiming space is not only a powerful artistic statement but also a radical way of building a community. (   )

7. The show "Nothing to Lose" by fatties was coldly received and severely criticized by the audience. (   )

PART FIVE
Questions

Watch the TED talk "Enough with the Fear of Fat" by Kelli Jean Drinkwater for the second time, answer the following questions, and then share your opinions with your partner or the whole class.

1. What does "fat phobia" refer to?

2. According to Kelli, what are the general biases against being fat/fat people? Do you think they are fair?

3. Why does Kelli believe that we should question the antifat bias?

4. What are radical body activists' attitudes towards themselves and their fattiness?

5. What are the activities that Kelli has engaged in as a radical fat activist?

6. What was the outcome of the show "Nothing to Lose" by people of size?

7. Do you think fat phobia exists in our society? If so, what are the consequences? Could you figure out some ways to combat fat phobia?

PART SIX
Spot dictation

Listen to some audio clips and fill in the blanks with the words or phrases you hear.

UNIT 10 Fat Phobia

1. I'm here today to talk to you about a very powerful little word, one that people will do almost anything to avoid becoming. Billion-dollar industries _____ because of the fear of it, and those of us who _____ are it are left to _____ a _____ storm surrounding it.

2. Let's not _____ it. I am the _____ F-A-T kind of fat. I am the elephant in the room. When I walked out on stage, some of you may have been thinking, "Aww, this is going to be _____, because everybody knows that fat people are funny".

3. This antifat bias has become so _____, so _____ to how we value ourselves and each other that we rarely question why we have such _____ for people of size and where that _____ comes from.

4. And through it all, that fierce little six-year-old has stayed with me, and she has helped me stand before you today as an _____ fat person, a person that simply refuses to _____ to the _____ narrative about how I should move through the world in this body of mine.

5. The impact of seeing a bunch of _____ fat women in _____ swimming caps and throwing their legs in the air without a care should not be _____.

6. I've even been called "the ISIS of the _____ epidemic" —a comment so absurd that it is funny. But it also speaks to the _____, the _____ terror, that the fear of fat can _____.

7. Fat activism refuses to _____ this fear. By _____ for _____ and respect for all of us, we can shift society's _____ to embrace diversity and start to celebrate the _____ ways there are to have a body.

PART SEVEN
Sentence study

Read the following sentences and understand their meanings. Pay attention to the bold faced and italic words and phrases.

1. Billion-dollar industries thrive because of the fear of it, and those of us who undeniably are it are left to **navigate** a *relentless* storm surrounding it.

2. Let's not *sugarcoat* it. I am the capital F-A-T kind of fat. I am the elephant in the room. When I walked out on stage, some of you may have been thinking, "Aww, this is going to be *hilarious*, because everybody knows that fat people are funny".

3. This antifat bias has become so *integral*, so *ingrained* to how we value ourselves and each other that we rarely question why we have such contempt for people of size and where that *disdain* comes from.

4. And do we really want to live in a society where people are denied their basic humanity if they don't *subscribe to* some *arbitrary* form of acceptable?

5. I soon learned that living outside what the mainstream considers normal can be a frustrating and isolating place. I've spent the last 20 years unpacking and *deprogramming* these messages, and it's been quite the *roller coaster.*

6. And these people have taught me that radical body politics is the *antidote* to our body-shaming culture.

7. And *reclaiming* spaces *en masse* is not only a powerful artistic statement but a radical community-building approach.

8. Throughout my career, I have learned that fat bodies are inherently political, and unapologetic fat bodies can *blow people's minds*.

UNIT 10 Fat Phobia

9. "Nothing to Lose" is a work made *in collaboration with* performers of size who drew from their lived experiences to create a work as varied and authentic as we all are.

PART EIGHT
Reading

Read the following quotes and share with others your understanding of them.

1. You can be fat and still be sexy. It all depends on how you feel about yourself. (Elizabeth Taylor)

2. Fat people are so rarely included in visual culture that fat is perceived as a blot on the landscape of sleek and slim. (Susie Orbach)

3. Healthy emotions come in all sizes. Healthy minds come in all sizes. And healthy bodies come in all sizes. (Cheri K. Erdman)

4. Losing weight is not your life's work, and counting calories is not the call of your soul. You surely are destined for something much greater. (Anonymous)

5. Girls of all kinds can be beautiful—from the thin, plus-sized, short, very tall, ebony to porcelain-skinned; the quirky, clumsy, shy, outgoing and all in between. It's not easy though because many people still put beauty into a confining, narrow box… Think outside of the box… Pledge that you will look in the mirror and find the unique beauty in you. (Tyra Banks)

6. So instead of beating myself up for being fat, I think it's a miracle that I laugh every day and walk through my life with pride, because our culture is unrelenting when it comes to large people. (Camryn Manheim)

7. Feed kids Cokes and French fries and you get an obesity crisis. Feed them mental junk food and you get non-readers and poor thinkers. (Joy Hakim)

UNIT 11
Positivity

PART ONE
Vocabulary

weaponry	all the weapons of a particular type or belonging to a particular country or group
cavalry	(in the past) the part of the army that fought on horses; the part of the modern army that uses armored vehicles
charge	a sudden rush or violent attack, for example by soldiers, wild animals or players in some sports
befall	(of sth. unpleasant) to happen to sb.
sniper	a person who shoots at sb. from a hidden position
wail	a long loud high cry expressing pain or sadness
erupt	to suddenly express your feelings very strongly, esp. by shouting loudly
avert	to prevent sth. bad or dangerous from happening
unicorn	(in stories) an animal like a white horse with a long straight horn on its head
vanguard	the part of an army, etc. that is at the front when moving forward to attack the enemy
academia	the world of learning, teaching, research, etc. at universities, and the people involved in it
weirdo	a person who looks strange and/or behaves in a strange way
eliminate	to remove or get rid of sb./sth.

cult	(~ of sth.) a way of life, an attitude, an idea, etc. that has become very popular
resiliency	the ability of people or things to feel better quickly after sth. unpleasant, such as shock, injury, etc.
glean	to obtain information, knowledge, etc., sometimes with difficulty and often from various different places
syndrome	a set of physical conditions that show you have a particular disease or medical problem
leprosy	an infectious disease that causes painful white areas on the skin and can destroy nerves and flesh
menopause	the time which a woman gradually stops menstruating, usu. at around the age of 50
hassles	a situation that is annoying because it involves doing sth. difficult or complicated that needs a lot of effort
disorder	an illness that causes a part of the body to stop functioning correctly
illicit	not allowed by the law
downturn	a fall in the amount of business that is done; a time when the economy becomes weaker
undergird	to provide support or a firm basis for
goalpost	one of the two vertical posts that form part of a goal
dopamine	a chemical produced by nerve cells which has an effect on other cells

PART TWO
Background information

Shawn Achor: He is the CEO of Good Think Inc., a Cambridge-based firm that researches people above average to understand the connection of human potential, success and happiness, in which he is one of the world leading experts. He is the author of *New York Times* bestselling books *The Happiness Advantage* (2010) and *Big Potential* (2018).

UNIT 11 Positivity

Positive Psychology: It is a relatively new subfield of psychology that focuses on the character strengths and behaviors that allow individuals to lead a meaningful, purposeful and flourishing life. Its proponents have sought to identity elements of good life and proposed practices that can improve individuals' life satisfaction and well-being. While there is some overlap with other branches of psychology, the primary concern of positive psychology is to help individuals identify and build mental assets, rather than address and repair their weaknesses and problems as other schools of psychology do. However, positive psychology is often criticized for focusing on positive experiences at the expense of negative ones.

Medical School Syndrome: Also referred to as "Medical Students' Disease", "Medical Student Disorder", it is a collection of signs and symptoms that a medical school student believes he or she has while studying a particular threatening disease in medical school. It is associated with an irrational fear of contracting a certain disease.

PART THREE
Warm-up questions

> Discuss the following question with your partner and then share your opinions with the whole class.

In your opinion, how can we build a positive and optimistic mindset?
_____
_____

PART FOUR
True or false statements

> Watch the TED talk "The Happy Secret to Better Work" by Shawn Achor for the first time and decide whether the following statements are true or false.

TED演讲视听说 2

1. The seven-year-old Shawn pushed his five-year-old sister off the top of their bunk bed, which resulted in the latter's breaking one of her legs. (   )

2. Psychologists of positivity study people high above the average level, gather information from them, and then help the average people move up. (   )

3. The majority of the information on the news is negative: about murder, corruption, diseases and natural disasters. (   )

4. Harvard students always feel happy and privileged to get into the school. (   )

5. A person's IQ can predict 75% of their job successes, whereas their optimism levels, social support and ability to see stress as a challenge instead of a threat can predict 25% of them. (   )

6. Generally speaking, our brains at positive are more productive and efficient than our brains at negative are. (   )

7. By writing down three new things they are grateful for for 21 days in a row, and by the end of it, people can form a pattern of seeing the world for the positive in their brains. (   )

PART FIVE
Questions

Watch the TED talk "The Happy Secret to Better Work" by Shawn Achor for the second time, answer the following questions, and then share your opinions with your partner or the whole class.

1. What happened to Shawn's five-year-old sister when they were playing a war game? How did he console his sister? And what was the result? How was this incident related to positive psychology?

2. What is the difference between positive psychology and traditional schools of psychology when encountering people above the average level (the positive outliers)?

UNIT 11 Positivity

3. What are Harvard college students' focuses after two weeks of their entering the university?
   _____
   _____

4. According to Shawn, what are the factors that predict a person's long-term happiness level?
   _____
   _____

5. From Shawn's investigation, what is most companies and schools' formula for happiness and success? Why does he believe that this formula is scientifically broken and backwards? What is positive psychology's formula for happiness and success?
   _____
   _____

6. What has Shawn suggested us to do to train our brain to be more positive?
   _____
   _____

7. Shawn says that, "We're finding it's not necessarily the reality that shapes us, but the lens through which your brain views the world that shapes your reality. And if we can change the lens, not only can we change your happiness, we can change every single educational and business outcome at the same time". Please share with others your understanding of the quote and elaborate it with examples.
   _____
   _____

PART SIX
Spot dictation

Listen to some audio clips and fill in the blanks with the words or phrases you hear.

1. And I saw my sister's face, this _____ of pain and suffering and surprise threatening to _____ from her mouth and wake my parents from the long winter's _____ for which they had settled. So I did the only thing my _____ seven year-old brain could think to do to _____ this tragedy.

89

2. And you could see how my poor, _____ sister faced conflict, as her little brain attempted to _____ resources to feeling the pain and suffering and surprise she just experienced, or _____ her new-found identity as a unicorn. And the latter won. Instead of crying or _____ our play, instead of waking my parents, with all the negative consequences for me, a smile spread across her face and she _____ back up onto the bunk bed with all the _____ of a baby unicorn—with one broken leg.

3. So one of the first things we teach people in economics, _____, business and psychology courses is how, in a statistically _____ way, do we eliminate the _____. How do we eliminate the _____ so we can find the line of best fit?

4. Why are some of you high above the _____ in terms of intellectual, athletic, musical ability, creativity, energy levels, _____ in the face of challenge, sense of humor? Whatever it is, instead of _____ you, what I want to do is study you. Because maybe we can _____ information, not just how to move people up to the average, but move the entire average up in our companies and schools worldwide.

5. Here's how we get to health: We need to _____ the formula for happiness and success. In the last three years, I've traveled to 45 countries, working with schools and companies in the midst of an economic _____. And I found that most companies and schools follow a formula for success, which is this: If I work harder, I'll be more successful. And if I'm more successful, then I'll be happier. That _____ most of our parenting and managing styles, the way that we _____ our behavior.

PART SEVEN
Sentence study

Read the following sentences and understand their meanings. Pay attention to the bold faced and italic words and phrases.

1. I nervously peered over the side of the bed to see what had **befallen** my fallen sister and saw that she had landed painfully on her hands and knees **on all fours** on the ground.

UNIT 11 Positivity

2. I was nervous because my parents **had charged me with** making sure that my sister and I played as safely and as quietly as possible.

3. And I saw my sister's face, this **wail** of pain and suffering and surprise threatening to **erupt** from her mouth and wake my parents from the long winter's nap for which they had settled. So I did the only thing my frantic seven year-old brain could think to do to **avert** this tragedy.

4. What we **stumbled across** at this tender age of just five and seven—we had no idea at the time—was going be at the **vanguard** of a scientific revolution occurring two decades later in the way that we look at the human brain.

5. So one of the first things we teach people in economics, statistics, business and psychology courses is how, in a statistically valid way, do we **eliminate** the **weirdos**. How do we eliminate the **outliers** so we can find the line of best fit?

6. Whatever it is, instead of deleting you, what I want to do is study you. Because maybe we can **glean** information, not just how to move people up to the average, but move the entire average up in our companies and schools worldwide.

7. I applied to Harvard *on a dare*.

8. I found that most companies and schools follow a formula for success, which is this: If I work harder, I'll be more successful. And if I'm more successful, then I'll be happier. That **undergirds** most of our parenting and managing styles, the way that we motivate our behavior.

PART EIGHT
Reading

> Read the following quotes and share with others your understanding of them.

1. Keep your face to the sunshine and you cannot see a shadow. (Helen Keller)

2. The joy of life comes from our encounters with new experiences, and hence there is no greater joy than to have an endlessly changing horizon, for each day to have a new and different sun. (Christopher McCandless)

3. Believe that life is worth living and your belief will help create the fact. (William James)

4. You've done it before and you can do it now. See the positive possibilities. Redirect the substantial energy of your frustration and turn it into positive, effective, unstoppable determination. (Ralph Marston)

5. Few things in the world are more powerful than a positive push. A smile. A world of optimism and hope. A "you can do it" when things are tough. (Richard M. DeVos)

6. Dream small dreams. If you make them too big, you get overwhelmed and you don't do anything. If you make small goals and accomplish them, it gives you the confidence to go on to higher goals. (John H. Johnson)

UNIT 11 Positivity

7. Building a practice of gratitude is the best way I know to create an optimistic approach to life. Start each day by lying in bed for five minutes and mentally acknowledging what you are grateful for. (Silken Laumann)

8. The optimist lives on the peninsula of infinite possibilities; the pessimist is stranded on the island of perpetual indecision. (William Arthur Ward)

9. It's not that optimism solves all of life's problems; it is just that it can sometimes make the difference between coping and collapsing. (Lucy MacDonald)

10. It is only in our darkest hours that we may discover the true strength of the brilliant light within ourselves that can never, ever, be dimmed. (Doe Zantamata)

11. The greatest glory in living lies not in never failing, but in rising every time we fail. (Nelson Mandela)

12. Your attitude is like a box of crayons that color your world. Constantly color your picture gray, and your picture will always be bleak. Try adding some bright colors to the picture by including humor, and your picture begins to lighten up. (Allen Klein)

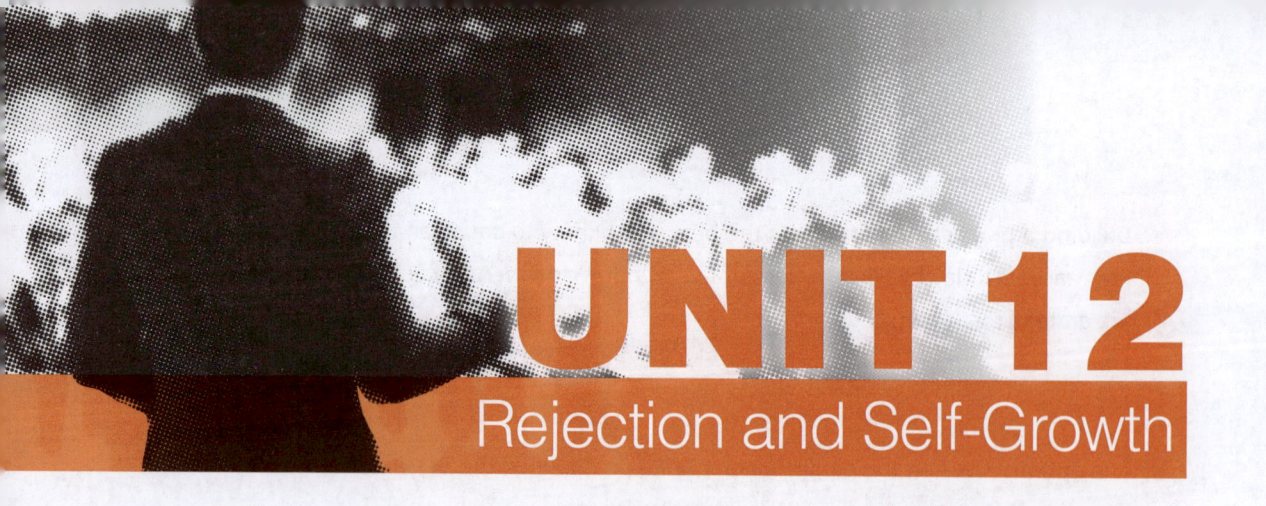

UNIT 12
Rejection and Self-Growth

PART ONE
Vocabulary

virtue	a particular good quality or habit
hearty	showing friendly feelings for sb.
roast	negative criticism, mockery
domination	authority to rule or control
stagnant	static, not developing, growing or changing
therapy	the treatment of a physical problem or an illness
desensitize	to treat sb./sth. so that they will stop being sensitive to physical or chemical changes, or to a particular substance
menacing	threatening, seeming likely to cause you harm or danger
microcosm	a thing, place or group that has all the features and qualities of sth. much larger
notoriety	fame for being bad in some way
referral	(~ to sb./sth.) sending sb. who needs professional help to a person or place that can provide it
maximize	to make the best use of sth.
demeanor	the way that sb. looks or behaves
trajectory	the curved path of sth.
curriculum	the subjects comprising a course of study in a school or college
boogeyman	an imaginary evil spirit used to frighten children

UNIT 12 Rejection and Self-Growth

PART TWO
Background information

Jia Jiang: He grew up in Beijing, China and emigrated to the U.S. when he was 16. He experienced failure in the corporate world and was in a deep self-doubt for a period of time. He realized that his fear of rejection was the biggest obstacle for success and he needed to overcome it, so he did an experiment, during which he voluntarily sought rejection on a daily basis. In 2015, he published a bestselling book *Rejection Proof: How I Beat Fear and Become Invincible Through 100 Days of Rejection* and in it he gives thoughtful suggestions of overcoming our fear and living more boldly and confidently.

PART THREE
Warm-up questions

> Discuss the following question with your partner and then share your opinions with the whole class.

Have you ever been rejected by others? If so, share with your partner your stories of getting rejected and your feelings of and reactions to rejections.

_____
_____

PART FOUR
True or false statements

> Watch the TED talk "What I Learned from 100 Days of Rejection" by Jia Jiang for the first time and decide whether the following statements are true or false.

1. As a six-year-old boy, Jia was the only student without getting compliments from his classmates. (   )

2. There were two versions of Jia battling with each other constantly and the version of himself as a 14-year-old boy wanting to conquer the world always won. (   )

3. The basic idea of "Rejection Therapy" game is that if you get rejected at something for 30 days in a row, you will desensitize from the pain of rejection by the end. (   )

4. During his rejection game of "Borrowing 100 Dollars from Stranger", Jia was scared and looked like he saw dead people. (   )

5. Jia wanted to plant a flower in a stranger's backyard but got refused, because the stranger did not love flowers. (   )

6. If you face rejections, you can embrace them and turn them into opportunities and gifts. (   )

PART FIVE
Questions

Watch the TED talk "What I Learned from 100 Days of Rejection" by Jia Jiang for the second time, answer the following questions, and then share your opinions with your partner or the whole class.

1. What was Jia's experience of being rejected as a six-year-old boy? How has that rejection influenced him?

2. What are the two versions of Jia? How did they interact with each other?

3. How did Jia come up with the idea of getting rejected for 100 days?

UNIT 12 Rejection and Self-Growth

4. What are some of Jia's rejection experiences? What are his lessons from them?
   _____
   _____

5. What are some lessons we can draw from this talk? In the future how will you cope with rejections and turn them into opportunities for self-growth?
   _____
   _____

PART SIX
Spot dictation

Listen to some audio clips and fill in the blanks with the words or phrases you hear.

1. My first grade teacher had this brilliant idea. She wanted us to experience receiving gifts but also learning the _____ of _____ each other.

2. She must have realized that she turned a team-building event into a public _____ for three six-year-olds.

3. I totally embraced this idea of _____ the world—_____, right? And I didn't make this up, I did write that letter.

4. I was actually a marketing manager for a *Fortune* 500 company. And I felt I was _____; I was _____.

5. But then I saw this guy. You know, he wasn't that _____. He was a _____, loveable guy, and he even asked me "why".

6. I felt, wow, this is like a _____ of my life. Every time I felt the slightest rejection, I would just run as fast as I could.

7. And I also learned that I can actually say certain things and _____ my chance to get a yes.

8. By the way, I don't know what your career _____ is, don't be a greeter.

9. And we don't have to be those people to learn about rejection, and in my case, rejection was my _____, was my _____.

PART SEVEN
Sentence study

Read the following sentences and understand their meanings. Pay attention to the bold faced and italic words and phrases.

1. And the teacher was *freaking out*. She was like, "Hey, would anyone say anything nice about these people?"

2. She must have realized that she turned a team-building event into a public *roast* for three six-year-olds.

3. I totally *embraced* this idea of *conquering* the world—domination, right?

4. And I felt I was *stuck*; I was *stagnant*.

5. Would any successful entrepreneur quit like that? No way. And this is where it *clicked* for me.

6. And basically the idea is for 30 days you go out and look for rejection, and every day get rejected at something, and then by the end, you *desensitize* yourself from the pain.

UNIT 12 Rejection and Self-Growth

7. I felt, wow, this is like a *microcosm* of my life. Every time I felt the slightest rejection, I would just run as fast as I could.

8. And then Day Three: Getting Olympic Doughnuts. This is where my life was *turned upside down*.

9. So she put out paper, started *jotting down* the colors and the rings, and is like, "How can I make this?"

10. But you know, fame and *notoriety* did not do anything to me. What I really wanted to do was to learn, and to change myself.

11. He's like, "Yeah, it's really weird, man." But as soon as he said that, his whole *demeanor* changed. It's as if he's putting all the doubt on the floor.

12. And in my case, rejection was my *curse*, was my *boogeyman*. It has bothered me my whole life because I was running away from it.

PART EIGHT
Reading

Read the following quotes and share with others your understanding of them.

1. Rejection puts you out of your comfort zone which is usually when you're at your best. (Stewart Stafford)

2. A clear rejection is better than a fake promise. (Leonardo DiCaprio)

3. If you live for people's acceptance you will die from their rejection. (Lecrae Moor)

4. I always feel like rejection is my petrol. That's what keeps me going. (Laura Kightlinger)

5. Every time I thought I was being rejected from something good, I was actually being redirected to something better. (Steve Maraboli)

6. Rejection doesn't have to mean you aren't good enough; it often just means the other person failed to notice what you have to offer. (Ash Sweeney)

7. Rejection isn't failure. Failure is giving up. Everyone gets rejected. It's how handle it that determines where you'll end up. (Richard Castle)

8. Rejection is a common occurrence. Learning that early and often will help you build up the tolerance and resistance to keep going and keep trying. (Kevin Feige)

UNIT 12 Rejection and Self-Growth

9. Every candle that gets lit in the dark room must feel a little rejection from the darkness around it, but the last thing I want from those who hold a different world view to me is to accept me. (Kirk Cameron)

10. The biggest hurdle is rejection. Any business you start, be ready for it. The difference between successful people and unsuccessful people is the successful people do all the things the unsuccessful people don't want to do. When 10 doors are slammed in your face, go to door number 11 enthusiastically, with a smile on your face. (John Paul DeJoria)

11. I take rejection as someone blowing a bugle in my ear to wake me up and get going, rather than retreat. (Sylvester Stallone)

12. Authors by the hundreds can tell you stories by the thousands of those rejection slips before they found a publisher who was willing to "gamble" on an unknown. (Zig Ziglar)

UNIT 13
Big Data and Thick Data

PART ONE
Vocabulary

oracle	(in ancient Greece) a place where people could go to ask the gods for advice or information about the future; the priest or priestess through whom the gods were thought to give their message
trance	a half-conscious state characterized by an absence of response to external stimuli, typically as induced by hypnosis or entered by a medium
prophecy	a statement that sth. will happen in the future, esp. one made by sb. with religious or magic powers
ethnographer	a person who studies different races and cultures
vendor	a person who sells things, for example food or newspapers, usu. outside on the street
qualitative	relating to, measuring, or measured by the quality of sth. rather than its quantity
entice	to persuade sb./sth. to go somewhere or to do sth., usu. by offering them sth.
knock-off	a copy or imitation, esp. of an expensive product
holistic	considering a whole thing or being to be more than a collection of parts
fad	a craze, an intense and widely shared enthusiasm for sth., esp. one that is short-lived
optimize	to make sth. as good as it can be

UNIT 13 Big Data and Thick Data

dynamics	(pl.) the way in which people or things behave and react to each other in a particular situation
unfathomable	too strange or difficult to be understood
quantify	to describe or express sth. as an amount or a number
fixated	(~ on sb./sth.) always thinking and talking about sb./sth. in a way that is not normal
appealing	attractive or interesting
babble	to talk quickly in a way that is difficult to understand
hallucinate	to see or hear things that are not really there because of illness or drugs
woozy	feeling unsteady, confused and unable to think clearly
inquisitor	a person who asks a lot of difficult questions
invalid	not based on all the facts, and therefore not correct
meaty	containing a lot of important or interesting ideas
binge	(~ on sth.) to eat or drink too much, esp. without being able to control yourself
verify	to check that sth. is true or accurate
validate	to prove that sth. is true
integrate	to combine two or more things so that they work together
automate	to use machine and computers instead of people to do a job or task

PART TWO
Background information

Tricia Wang: She is a technology ethnographer and co-founder of Constellate Data, a company providing research and training for organizations that use data to understand people. She also gives corporations advice on how to use thick data—to use qualitative ethnographic research methods to reveal stories, human emotions and deeper meanings—to improve policies, performances, services and products. She got Ph.D. of sociology from University of California at San Diego.

Mayan calendar: It is an ancient calendar system dating back at least to the 5th century BCE and is still used by some Mayan communities in Central America today. It is made up of three corresponding calendars—the Haab, the Tzolkin and the Long Count—and they should be used simultaneously. The Haab is a 365-day solar calendar and is divided into 19 months. The Tzolkin is the sacred calendar with 260-day for 20 periods, and 13 days for each period. The Long Count is an astronomical calendar to track long periods of time and is made up of 2,880,000 days. This calendar is used for religious and ceremonious events.

Nokia: It is a Finnish telecommunications, information technology and consumer electronics company. Established in 1865, it has had various industries and has been associated with different types of products during its long history. Since the 1990s, it mainly concentrates on telecommunications infrastructure and new technology and is most famous for its mobile phones.

Netflix: It is an American media services provider, founded in 1997 in Scotts Valley, California. It offers online stream of films and television programs. In 2012, Netflix expanded its business and entered content-production industry, with its debut series *Lilyhammer*. In January 2019, it reached 1.39 billion paid subscribers worldwide.

PART THREE
Warm-up questions

Discuss the following question with your partner and then share your opinions with the whole class.

With the development of technology and advent of new channels for communication, large quantities of data have been generated and collected, and "big data" has become a buzzword and been widely circulated and used. What are some of the applications of big data? What do you think are the merits and demerits of big data?

UNIT 13 Big Data and Thick Data

PART FOUR
True or false statements

> Watch the TED talk "The Human Insights Missing from Big Data" by Tricia Wang for the first time and decide whether the following statements are true or false.

1. Today big data is regarded as our oracle, for we would like to get answers from them to a lot of important questions. (　)

2. The big data industry is a big one as the returns are surprisingly high and the majority of big data projects are profitable. (　)

3. Through her research in China, Tricia realized that even some poorest Chinese would like to have a smartphone and would do almost whatever they could to get one. (　)

4. Big data's success comes from quantifying systems, which also explains its weakness, because systems are often dynamic and can't be easily quantified. (　)

5. In ancient Greece, the oracle worked alone, without any help from temple guides. (　)

6. Big data systems give invalid predictions, so they need to be integrated with thick data. (　)

PART FIVE
Questions

> Watch the TED talk "The Human Insights Missing from Big Data" by Tricia Wang for the second time, answer the following questions, and then share your opinions with your partner or the whole class.

1. What was Tricia's insight about smartphone? Why was Nokia not convinced by it?

2. Why is having big data won't necessarily help people make better decisions? What are the problems of big data?
   _____
   _____

3. What is quantification bias? Can you cite examples of quantification bias in our daily life?
   _____
   _____

4. What did Netflix do to avoid shortcomings of big data?
   _____
   _____

5. What is thick data? What are its characteristics? Why should big data be integrated with thick data?
   _____
   _____
   _____

6. Giving the demerits of big data, how should we use it to our advantage?
   _____
   _____

PART SIX
Spot dictation

> Listen to some audio clips and fill in the blanks with the words or phrases you hear.

1. In ancient Greece, when anyone, from slaves to soldiers, poets and politicians, needed to make a big decision on life's most important questions, like, "Should I get married?" or "Should we _____ this voyage?" or "Should our army advance into this _____?" they all consulted the _____.

2. From the oracle bones of ancient China to ancient Greece to Mayan _____, people have _____ for _____ in order to find out what's going to happen next.

UNIT 13 Big Data and Thick Data

3. Your surveys, your methods have been designed to _____ an existing business model, and I'm looking at these _____ human _____ that haven't happened yet.

4. Big data's _____ for success comes from quantifying very specific environments, like electricity power_____ or delivery _____ or genetic code, when we're quantifying in systems that are more or less _____.

5. But Netflix discovered the improvements were only _____. So to really find out what was going on, they hired an _____, Grant McCracken, to gather thick data insights.

PART SEVEN
Sentence study

> Read the following sentences and understand their meanings. Pay attention to the bold faced and italic words and phrases.

1. From the oracle bones of ancient China to ancient Greece to Mayan calendars, people have **craved for** prophecy in order to find out what's going to happen next.

2. What are **the odds** of my child being born with a genetic disorder?

3. I found out that the ads that actually **enticed** them the most were the ones for iPhones, promising them this entry into this high-tech life.

4. I saw people investing over half of their monthly income into buying a phone, and increasingly, they were "shanzhai", which are affordable **knock-offs** of iPhones and other brands.

5. Your surveys, your methods have been designed to *optimize* an existing business model, and I'm looking at these emergent human *dynamics* that haven't happened yet.

6. People become so *fixated on* that number, that they can't see anything outside of it, even when you present them evidence right in front of their face.

7. But the problem is that quantifying is addictive. And when we forget that and when we don't have something to kind of *keep* that *in check*, it's very easy to just throw out data because it can't be expressed as a numerical value.

8. Oftentimes, the future we need to predict—it isn't in that haystack, but it's that tornado that's *bearing down on* us outside of the barn.

9. So Netflix was like, "Oh. This is a new insight." So they went to their data science team, and they were able to *scale* this big data insight in with their quantitative data. And once they *verified* it and *validated* it, Netflix decided to do something very simple but *impactful*.

PART EIGHT
Reading

Read the following quotes and share with others your understanding of them.

UNIT 13 Big Data and Thick Data

1. You can have data without information, but you cannot have information without data. (Daniel Keys Moran)

2. Without big data analytics, companies are blind and deaf, wandering out onto the web like deer on a freeway. (Geoffrey Moore)

3. Consumer data will be the biggest differentiator in the next two to three years. Whoever unlocks the reams of data and uses it strategically will win. (Angela Ahrendts)

4. Errors using inadequate data are much less than those using no data at all. (Charles Babbage)

5. You can use all the quantitative data you can get, but you still have to distrust it and use your own intelligence and judgment. (Alvin Toffler)

6. Data is the new science. Big data holds the answers. (Pat Gelsinger)

7. Data scientists are involved with gathering data, massaging it into a tractable form, making it tell its story, and presenting that story to others. (Mike Loukides)

8. It is a capital mistake to theorize before one has data. (Arthur Conan Doyle)

9. There were 5 exabytes of information created between the dawn of civilization through 2003, but that much information is now created every 2 days. (Eric Schmidt)

UNIT 14
Human Skin Colors and Revolution

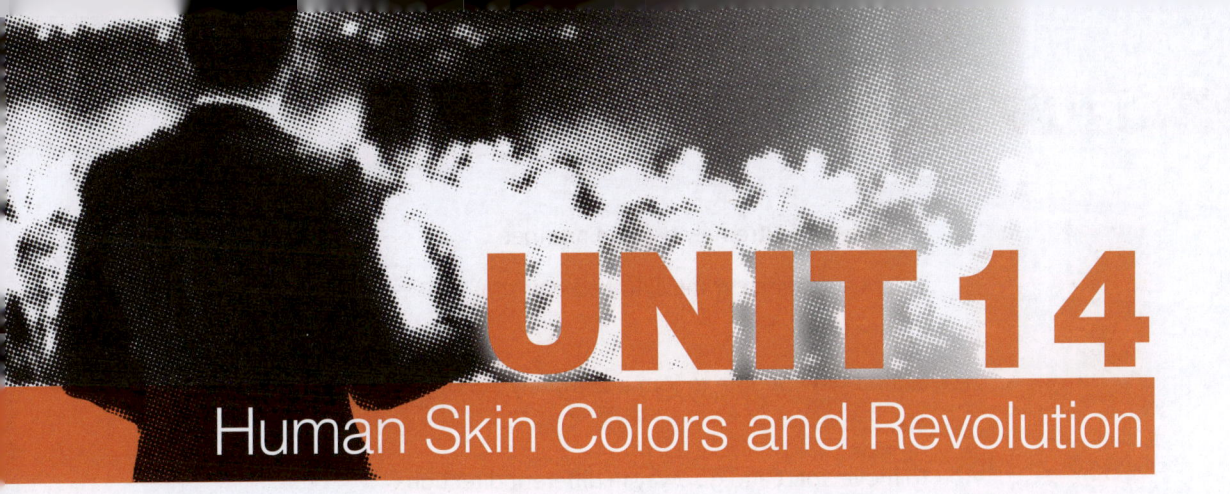

PART ONE
Vocabulary

pigment	a substance that exists naturally in people, animals and plants and gives their skin, leaves, etc. a particular color; color sth. with pigment
pigmentation	the presence of pigments in skin, hair, leaves, etc. that causes them to be a particular color
distill	to get the essential meaning or ideas from thoughts, information, experiences, etc.
infamous	well known for being bad or evil
increment	an increase in a number or an amount
conspicuous	easy to see or notice; likely to attract attention
gradient	the rate at which temperature, pressure, etc. changes, or increases and decreases, between one region and another
equator	(usu. the equator) an imaginary line around the Earth at an equal distance from the North and South Poles
lineage	the series of families that sb. comes from originally
bombard	to attack (a place or person) continuously with bombs, shells, or other missiles
occlude	to cover or block sth.
unimpeded	with nothing blocking or stopping sb./sth.
catalyze	to cause (an action or process) to begin

111

myriad	countless or extremely great in number
melanin	a dark substance in the skin and hair that causes the skin to change color in the sun's light
recruit	to find new people to join a company, an organization, the armed forces, etc.
disperse	to move apart and go away in different directions
dissipate	to gradually become or make sth. become weaker until it disappears
bereft	(~ of sth.) complete lacking sth.; having lost sth.
testament	(~ to sth.) a thing that shows that sth. else exists or is true
transgress	to go beyond the limits of (what is morally, socially, or legally acceptable)
invidious	unpleasant and unfair; likely to offend sb. or make him/her jealous
deleterious	harmful and damaging
impediment	(~ to sth.) sth. that delays or stops the process of sth.
epidemiologist	a person who studies the spread and control of diseases
sinister	seeming evil or dangerous; making you think sth. bad will happen
proximity	(~ of/to sb./sth.) the state of being near sb. /sth. in distance or time
emblematic	(~ of sth.) that presents or is a symbol of sth.
tan	(~ sb./sth) to make a person's skin become brown as a result of spending time in the sun
eschew	to deliberately avoid or keep away from sth.

PART TWO
Background information

Nina Jablonski (1953–): She is Professor of Anthropology at the Pennsylvania State University. Renowned for her research on the evolution of human skin and skin pigmentation, she has frequently engaged in science education with the aim of enhancing the public understanding of human evolution, human diversity, and human racism. In 2021, she became a member of the America National Academy of Sciences. She has published two books regarding human skin color: *Skin: A Natural History* and *Living Color: The Biological and Social Meaning of Skin Color*.

UNIT 14 Human Skin Colors and Revolution

Charles Darwin (1809–1882): As a renowned British biologist, he is famous for his theory of evolution and natural selection. Between 1831 and 1836, he was on board the ship The HMS *Beagle* for his voyage around the world, which had a tremendous influence on his view of natural history. In 1859, he published his landmark book *On the Origin of Species*, in which he established his revolutionary and controversial theory of natural selection as the explanation of the diversity of life on the Earth. Darwin's evolutionary theory has changed countless fields, from biology to sociology, and from philosophy to anthropology.

Neanderthals: They are a group of ancient humans living at least 200,000 years ago. They inhabited in Eurasia, from the Atlantic region of Europe eastward to Central Asia, and the present-day Belgium southward to the Mediterranean and southwest Asia. Their fossils were first found in Neander Valley in Germany, hence their name Neanderthals. They lived in caves, developed complex stone tools for hunting and domestic uses, and became extinct between 35,000 and perhaps 24,000 years ago, probably due to the climate change.

PART THREE
Warm-up questions

Discuss the following questions with your partner and then share your opinions with the whole class.

1. For people of all races, how many skin colors are there in the world? What do you think are the possible reasons for such differing skin colors?

2. Do you know any prejudices against people of different skin colors? Why do you think such prejudices exist?

PART FOUR
True or false statements

> Watch the TED talk "Skin Color Is an Illusion" by Nina Jablonski for the first time and decide whether the following statements are true or false.

1. One weakness of Charles Darwin's *On the Origin of Species* is that it says nothing of the origin of humans and our history. (   )

2. Charles Darwin accepted the idea that human skin color was related to the climate and environment people living in. (   )

3. Much of the Northern Hemisphere receives the highest amounts of UV radiation. (   )

4. From the map of skin color we can see that the lightest skin pigmentations are toward the poles, and the darkest ones are toward the equator. (   )

5. UVB is totally useful, for it catalyzes the production of vitamin D in human skin. (   )

6. The melanin in our skin serves as a natural sunscreen. (   )

7. People inhabiting Northern Hemisphere lost the potential to make Vitamin B in their skin for most of the year, so they lost their pigmentation. (   )

8. Epidemiologists and doctors are good at teaching darkly pigmented people living in high latitude areas, or working inside all the time, how to protect their skin. (   )

PART FIVE
Questions

> Watch the TED talk "Skin Color Is an Illusion" by Nina Jablonski for the second time, answer the following questions, and then share your opinions with your partner or the whole class.

UNIT 14 Human Skin Colors and Revolution

1. What was Charles Darwin's observation of human skin color? What was his prejudice concerning it?

2. What did NASA discover about the radiation of the Earth's surface?

3. What is the function of the melanin?

4. According to Nina, what is the relationship between ultraviolent radiation and human skin color? How is human skin color related to evolution?

5. What are the problems people face if their skin colors are incompatible with their living environment?

6. What are your observations of people's attitudes towards skin color in our culture? What do you think should be our good attitudes towards our skin color?

PART SIX
Spot dictation

Listen to some audio clips and fill in the blanks with the words or phrases you hear.

1. Interestingly, Charles Darwin was born a very lightly pigmented man, in a moderately-to-darkly pigmented world. Over the course of his life, Darwin had great _____. He lived in a fairly wealthy home. He was raised by very supportive and interested parents. And when he was in his 20s he _____ upon a remarkable voyage on the ship the *Beagle*. And during the course of that voyage, he saw remarkable things: Tremendous _____ of plants and animals, and humans. And the observations that he made on that _____ journey were to be eventually _____ into his wonderful book, *On the _____ of Species*, published 150 years ago.

2. What's significant to the story of human skin pigmentation is just how much of the Northern _____ is in these cool gray zones. This has tremendous _____ for our understanding of the evolution of human skin pigmentation. And what Darwin could not appreciate, or didn't perhaps want to appreciate at the time, is that there was a fundamental relationship between the _____ of ultraviolet radiation and skin pigmentation. And that skin pigmentation itself was a product of _____.

3. So, living at the _____, we got lots and lots of ultraviolet radiation and the melanin—this wonderful, complex, ancient polymer _____ in our skin—served as a superb natural _____. This polymer is amazing because it's present in so many different _____. Melanin, in various forms, has probably been on the Earth a billion years, and has been _____ over and over again by evolution, as often happens.

4. Look at some of the major _____ _____: People from high UV areas going to low UV and _____. And not all these moves were _____. Between 1520 and 1867, 12 million, 500 people were moved from high UV to low UV areas in the transatlantic slave trade. Now this had all sorts of _____ social consequences. But it also had _____ health consequences to people.

PART SEVEN
Sentence study

Read the following sentences and understand their meanings. Pay attention to the bold faced and italic words and phrases.

UNIT 14   Human Skin Colors and Revolution

1. And the observations that he made on that *epic* journey were to be eventually *distilled* into his wonderful book, *On the Origin of Species*, published 150 years ago.

2. "Of all the differences between the races of men, the color of the skin is the most *conspicuous* and one of the best marked."… "These differences do not *coincide with* corresponding differences in climate."

3. The earliest members of our *lineage*, the genus Homo, were darkly pigmented. And we all share this incredible *heritage* of having originally been darkly *pigmented*, two million to one and half million years ago.

4. In those early days of our evolution, looking at the equator, we were *bombarded* by high levels of ultraviolet radiation. The UVC, the most energetic type, was *occluded* by the Earth's atmosphere. But UVB and UVA especially, came in *unimpeded*.

5. UVB turns out to be incredibly important. It's very destructive, but it also *catalyzes* the production of Vitamin D in the skin, Vitamin D being a molecule that we very much need for our strong bones, the health of our immune system, and *myriad* other important functions in our bodies.

6. And humans *dispersed*—not once, but twice.

7. So people inhabiting northern hemispheric environments *were bereft of* the potential to make Vitamin D in their skin for most of the year.

8. Look at some of the major latitudinal *transgressions*: People from high UV areas going to low UV and vice versa. And not all these moves were *voluntary*. Between 1520 and 1867, 12 million, 500 people were moved from high UV to low UV areas in the transatlantic slave trade. Now this had all sorts of *invidious* social consequences. But it also had *deleterious* health consequences to people.

9. Vitamin D deficiency *creeps up* on people, and causes all sorts of health problems to their bones, …

10. We live in a world where we have lightly and darkly pigmented people living next to one another, but often brought into *proximity* initially as a result of very invidious social interactions.

11. He, as one of many urban admixed populations, *is* very *emblematic of* a mixed parentage, of a mixed pigmentation.

12. Darwin, I think, would have appreciated this, even though he *eschewed* the importance of climate on the evolution of pigmentation during his own life.

PART EIGHT
Reading

Read the following quotes and share with others your understanding of them.

UNIT 14 — Human Skin Colors and Revolution

1. I'm not one that believes that affirmative action should be based on one's skin color or one's gender; I think it should be done based on one's need, because I think if you are from a poor white community, I think that poor white kid needs a scholarship just as badly as a poor black kid. (J. C. Watts)

2. Being able to live without having to be defined by your skin color is the hallmark of privilege. (Luvvie Ajayi)

3. When I was, like, 5 years old, I used to pray to have light skin because I would always hear how pretty that little light skin girl was, or I would hear I was pretty to be dark skin. It wasn't until I was 13 that I really learned to appreciate my skin color and know that I was beautiful. (Keke Palmer)

4. Take that one thing you don't like about yourself and more often than not that's the one thing that makes you more special. Whether it's that gap in your teeth, or that mole you never liked, or your skin color. (Shay Mitchell)

5. The Muslim world just doesn't believe that skin color is all that important. Obama may be half-black, but he's still all-Western, according to them. It doesn't matter whether you're black, white or green—if you're not a devotee of Muhammad, you don't matter. (Ben Shapiro)

6. Look at how lucky white people are compared to black people, who have suffered so much just because of their skin color, and then there are native people, who were the first people of this country and have suffered so much just because some newcomers came over and said: "Hey this looks like a nice place to set up camp. Just hand it over to us." (Severn Cullis-Suzuki)

7. There's something not right with a person's soul when they judge another human being to be less adequate because of their gender or skin color. (Lexi Alexander)

_____
_____

8. I don't care about the skin color, everybody is a human being. Beneath every skin color, you bleed red. That's just the bottom line of the truth. (Angelique Kidjo)

_____
_____